# Literacy Challenges

## for the more able

### a collection of mini projects

Shelagh Moore

# Book 4

HOPSCOTCH
EDUCATIONAL PUBLISHING

For Michael Kelliher
Headteacher and School Governor
A gifted and dedicated educator.

Published by
Hopscotch Educational Publishing Ltd
Unit 2
The Old Brushworks
56 Pickwick Road
Corsham
Wiltshire
SN13 9BX

01249 701701

© 2004 Hopscotch Educational Publishing

Written by Shelagh Moore
Series design by Blade Communications
Cover illustration by Sarah Wimperis
Illustrated by Sarah Wimperis
Printed by Colorman Ireland Ltd

ISBN 1-904307-11-6

**Acknowledgments**
The author and publisher gratefully acknowledge permission to reproduce copyright material in this book.
Extract from *Angela's Ashes* by Frank McCourt (HarperCollins Publishers Ltd) Copyright © 1996 Frank McCourt
Extract from *The Tulip Touch* by Anne Fine (Hamish Hamilton, 1996) Copyright © Anne Fine 1996
Extract from *Chains* by Frances Mary Hendry (OUP, 2000), copyright © Frances Mary Hendry 2000, reprinted by permission of Oxford University Press
Extract from *Watership Down* by Richard Adams published by Penguin Books, 1972. Copyright © Richard Adams 1072. Permission granted by David Higham Associates
Extract from *Redwall* by Brian Jacques published by Hutchinson 1986. Used by permission of the Random House Group Limited.

Every effort has been made to trace the owners of copyright of material in this book and the publisher apologises for any inadvertent omissions. Any persons claiming copyright for any material should contact the publisher who will be happy to pay the permission fees agreed between them and who will amend the information in this book on any subsequent reprint.

**Literacy**
*for the more able*

# Contents

# Introduction

## About the series

*Literacy Challenges* is a series of four books specifically targeted at the more able child in Key Stages 2 and 3. Each book contains ten challenges or mini projects that the teacher can introduce to the pupils who can then work independently, in pairs or small groups to complete the series of set tasks. Each project encourages the development of time management skills and independent research, culminating in a specific end product, such as a written report, a prepared presentation or a radio programme.

The first five challenges in each book are text-based projects where the pupils are encouraged to explore well-known stories and poems in a variety of genres. The second five challenges are more cross-curricular projects, designed to develop the pupils' reasoning and cognitive skills.

Each challenge is designed to take three to six weeks if timetabled on a twice-weekly basis or as part of extra-curricular work for the more able. The challenges do not need to be carried out in any particular order, although each one is matched to the objectives for each term of the *Literacy Framework* and can, therefore, be carried out in accordance with the required range for each term.

The books are aimed at specific National Curriculum English levels and *Literacy Framework* year groups but the challenges work well with children across the Key Stage 2 and Key Stage 3 age range.

Book 1: English NC levels 2–3; *Literacy Framework* – Year 3
Book 2: English NC levels 3–4; *Literacy Framework* – Year 4
Book 3: English NC levels 4–5; *Literacy Framework* – Year 5
Book 4: English NC levels 5–6; *Literacy Framework* – Year 6

## About each book

Each book contains ten challenges that are presented in a specific format – a section of teacher's notes and a collection of photocopiable pages that the teacher can provide for each pupil. (These photocopiable pages are listed in the 'Resources required' section of each challenge.)

### Teacher's notes
The teacher's notes contain the following information:

### Purposes
This outlines the expected learning outcomes for each challenge.

### Aims
This defines the aims of each challenge.

### Resources required
This lists the resources the teacher needs to provide the pupils with.

### The teacher's role
This provides the teacher with all the information she or he needs in order to introduce the challenge to the pupils, plus tips and hints on how to help them when they are using the photocopiable support sheets for each challenge. Links to the National Curriculum and *Literacy Framework* are also provided.

### The photocopiable sheets
The photocopiable sheets are intended to be used by the pupils. They could be stapled together (or put into a ring binder) to make a booklet for the pupil (with the **'Challenge sheet'** used as a cover page), thereby keeping all the materials together.

### 'My action planning sheet'
Action planning is an essential part of the challenge. The completion of the challenge may take about three to six weeks if the pupils are given only set times each week for working on their tasks. This sheet provides an opportunity for them to plan their work with definite starts, tasks and deadlines. The teacher needs to ensure that the pupils have planned out the tasks they are carrying out in a manner that is logical and will lead to successful completion of the unit. Completing the sheet immediately after the tasks have been read and discussed allows the pupil and teacher to plan a suitable sequence of work to agreed deadlines. The teacher is also able to plan visits and visitors using this sheet with the pupils.

The teacher's role is to help the pupils understand that action plans often need modification as the work progresses and that this is good practice, not a sign of failure. Pupils who are able to assess their own progress and adapt their planning tend to be those who have more success with completing the set tasks. Once they have planned their work, the real work (as they will see it) can begin!

### The 'Task sheets'
Each challenge is divided into two parts – 'Task sheet 1' and 'Task sheet 2'. 'Task sheet 1' contains a set of activities that prepares the pupil for 'Task sheet 2'. These activities often involve extensive reading, discussion and research. 'Task sheet 2' requires the pupils to use the information gathered in 'Task sheet 1' to write, make or prepare

something, such as an advertising poster, a talk to younger children or a story.

The teacher will need to discuss each stage of the task sheets with the pupils, making sure they understand what they need to do and how they are going to do it (the 'Planning guidelines' sheet goes into more detail for the pupil).

The task sheets are further supported by additional pupils' sheets (such as text mapping sheets and writing guides) that will enable them to carry out their research and plan and present their work.

## The 'Planning guidelines' and 'Resources' sheets

The 'Planning guidelines' provide the pupils with a useful summary of the tasks they have to complete. It includes helpful tips and reminders to help them in their planning.

The 'Resources' sheet provides ideas for research and suggests ways in which the pupils can gather information from a variety of sources. Planning the research and waiting for replies to queries is part of the pupil's action planning. Some tasks will not be easy to complete if speakers and visits are not organised in advance – this is where teacher guidance is valuable.

**IMPORTANT:** the teacher will need to ensure the pupils understand that they should not write to, contact or visit a potential source of information without the teacher's consent and guidance.

## Tha 'Mapping' and 'Discussion' sheets and 'Writing guides'

The various mapping and discussion sheets and writing guides enable the pupils to develop their skills in different aspects of speaking and listening, reading and writing. They should be used to help them to understand the structure of the tasks set and how to plan them. They 'map out' the thinking that should go into the planning of the tasks and provide a structured approach to their completion. Teachers and pupils can use the sheets to discuss the tasks and the content that is needed to complete them.

## The 'Skills sheets'

The skills sheets enable the pupil to identify the skills developed and practised while completing the challenges. They are generic documents that cover all the challenges and include subject areas that apply to the various tasks set. The pupil can read the sheets and identify the skills he or she feels that they have demonstrated. The pupil may feel that they have successfully demonstrated the skill or that they need more help with this type of skill. They can use the 'Skills sheets' to discuss their progress with their teacher.

## Assessment

An 'Assessment sheet' has been included for each challenge. It can be used by the teacher to identify the levels and skills achieved. The pupil will know from the assessment, which can be continuous throughout the unit of work, what level they are achieving and what they have still to achieve.

The teacher can use this assessment sheet as part of the pupil's record of work for final level assessments at the end of the academic year.

## Organisation

Although the challenges are designed to provide pupils with a self-contained unit of work that they can manage independently, it is essential that the teacher guides them through the whole process and tells them how much time will be allocated to the tasks each week.

Each challenge could form part of a whole class topic with separate work being planned for other pupils in the class. Alternatively it could form part of a regular weekly time slot allocated to the more able pupils in order for them to carry out independent work.

They will, however, need the teacher to guide them through the research work and help them make contact with those who can give them the help they need. The pupils should be encouraged to do their research and make any outside contacts under supervision in school.

Special consideration needs to be given to internet research to ensure that only child-suitable sites are used.

## Taking the challenges further

Pupils working on the units may well find that they want to develop a particular aspect of the work that interests them. This should be negotiated with the teacher and put into their planning so that they ensure that they complete the tasks set in the unit as well.

Units can be used to develop aspects of the curriculum that the pupils are studying in more depth and from a different perspective. The cross-curricular approach enables the pupils to see that their literacy skills can be applied effectively in other areas of the curriculum and that there are connections between different subjects that help them to understand them better.

# Challenge 1

# Radio Alpha

## Teacher's notes

### Purposes

- To evaluate a book.
- To find out about radio programmes and how they are made.
- To develop thinking, planning and time management skills.

### Aims

- To select a suitable book to be reviewed.
- To produce a radio programme about a review of a book of their choice for a specified audience.

### Resources required

The pupil will need copies of the following:

| | | |
|---|---|---|
| 1 | 'Challenge sheet' | page 112 |
| 2 | 'My action planning sheet' | page 113 |
| 3 | 'Task sheets' | pages 9 and 10 |
| 4 | 'Planning guidelines' | page 11 |
| 5 | 'Resources' sheet | page 12 |
| 6 | 'Text map' | page 13 |
| 7 | 'Character map' | page 14 |
| 8 | 'Report guide' | page 15 |
| 9 | 'Skills sheets' | page 114–117 |

### The teacher's role

#### 1 Introducing the challenge

Write the following in the top box of a copy of the 'Challenge sheet' (page 112):

*You are going to make a radio programme for Radio Alpha. The idea of the programme is to tell listeners about a book you have enjoyed recently. (The radio programme is planned to be presented in conjunction with Book Week.)*

*You need to select a suitable book, decide what type of audience you are aiming the programme at and then plan and produce the radio programme.*

Then photocopy the 'Challenge sheet' and give it to the pupils. Alternatively, they could be given a blank copy of the sheet and write the challenge on it themselves. It is important for them to have the challenge to refer to.

#### 2 Providing support for the task sheets

**Choosing a book**

Act as a guide in the selection of a book to use as a basis for the radio programme in order to ensure it is suitable.

Questions that could be asked include:

- *'Why would a radio audience particularly want to hear about this book?'*
- *'What is it about the book that you think will make them sit up and listen?'*

**Using the 'Text map'**

The 'Text map' enables the pupils to explore the main elements of the text quickly and effectively. The boxes on the sheet can simply be ticked or they can be used to record a page reference number where appropriate.

Explain the sheet to the pupils, making sure they understand what to do. Tell them that the character's role is the part played by character in the story. Discuss the text with the pupils – what they like about it and what aspects they would want to promote in the radio programme.

**Using the 'Character map'**

This sheet enables the pupils to investigate one of the characters in more detail to find out how they impact on the text as a whole.

Make sure the pupil understands the purpose of the mapping sheet and how it can help them plan their radio programme.

**Using the 'Report guide'**

This guide provides support for the pupils when they write their evaluation report about their radio programme. Make sure they understand what to do. Revise the correct layout of a report with its introduction, development and conclusion.

#### 3 Other points to note

The tasks on the 'Radio Alpha' sheets are straightforward, but to produce a 'proper' radio programme needs an understanding of the processes that go into making such a programme. The able pupil should be able to undertake thorough research and show interest in finding out about how a programme is made and what they need to do in order to achieve a professional sounding programme. They should be able to organise their tasks and to recognise the need to change their action plan if necessary to achieve their aims.

They will, however, need the teacher to guide them through the research work and help them make contact with those who can give them the help they need. The pupils should be encouraged to write their letters and make their phone calls under supervision in school. The pupil may need to listen to the radio programmes as a homework task. The teacher may also need to guide the pupil in selecting a suitable audience for the radio programme. Their journal (see 'Task sheet 2') should be a piece of writing that reflects their work and the problems they solved along the way.

Guidance may also need to be provided in selecting the most appropriate recording equipment (a simple cassette recorder will do) and a suitable place to make the recording (away from noises and distractions).

Finally, the programme, if possible, should be 'broadcast' to the specified audience and feedback given to help the pupils evaluate their programme in their report. The able pupil should be capable of learning from this unit that planning, research, preparation and time management are essential if there is to be a satisfactory outcome.

## Links to the National Curriculum

### English – Speaking and Listening

*Level 5: Pupils talk confidently in a wide range of contexts. They pay close attention to what others say, ask questions and develop ideas.*
*Level 6: Pupils adapt their talk to the demands of different contexts. They use a variety of vocabulary and expression. They take an active and positive part in discussion. They use language appropriate to the situation.*

### English – Reading

*Level 5: Pupils select essential points, they identify key features in their research and they use relevant information to support their views.*
*Level 6: Pupils refer to aspects of language and structure to prepare their script.*

### English – Writing

*Level 5: Pupils' writing conveys meaning clearly and is appropriate to the task set. Punctuation is generally accurate and handwriting is legible and cursive.*

*Level 6: Pupils' writing engages and sustains the reader's interest. The writing style is appropriate to the task set. Report writing uses an impersonal style. Punctuation is accurate and paragraphs are used correctly.*

## Links to Literacy Framework

### Year 6, Term 1

#### Word level work
*Vocabulary is extended through the use of specialist language relating to the task and can be used to compile a class dictionary of technical terms.*

#### Sentence level work
*S1 – to adapt writing for a particular audience.*

#### Text level work
*T3 – to articulate personal responses to literature, identifying why and how a text affects the reader.*
*T4 – to be familiar with the work of some established authors, to know what is special about their work, and to explain their preferences in terms of authors, styles and themes.*
*T5 – to contribute constructively to shared discussion about literature, responding to and building on the views of others.*

# Assessment sheet

Name: _____ Date: _____

| | Achieved | To achieve |
|---|---|---|

## Speaking and Listening:

**Level 5:**
- Talks confidently about the text, radio programmes and planning.
- Listens carefully to others.
- Asks questions and develops ideas.

**Level 6:**
- Adapts talk to the demands of different contexts with confidence.
- Uses a variety of vocabulary and expression.
- Uses language appropriate to the situation.

## Reading:

**Level 5:**
- Selects essential points in the text.
- Identifies key features, themes and characters in the text.
- Uses relevant information to support his or her views.

**Level 6:**
- Identifies layers of meaning in the chosen text.
- Gives a personal response to the text.
- Refers to aspects of language and structure when deciding the content of the radio script.

## Writing:

**Level 5:**
- Writing conveys meaning clearly.
- Writing is appropriate to the task set.
- Sentences are organised into paragraphs.
- Punctuation is accurate and handwriting legible.
- Handwriting is joined, clear and fluent.

**Level 6:**
- Writing engages and sustains the reader's interest.
- Ideas are organised into paragraphs.
- Punctuation is used to clarify meaning.
- Handwriting is joined, neat and legible.

# Task sheet 1

## Selecting a book

### Aim

To select a suitable book to be reviewed on a radio programme.

### Tasks

• Use the **My action planning sheet** to help you plan your work.

• **Choose a book** that you have read and enjoyed recently.

• With the help of your teacher, decide if the book would be a suitable one to discuss in a radio programme. Think carefully about whether or not you think other people will also be interested in hearing about this book and why.

• Map out the book using the **Text map sheet**.

• Complete the **Character map sheet**.

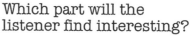
Which part will the listener find interesting?

• List the incidents in the book that you think will interest the listener. Do the parts you have chosen make a character interesting or the story exciting?

• Start to think about the audience for your radio programme.

Who will be listening?

Will they be your age, younger or older, or a mix of ages?

# Task sheet 2

## Making a radio programme

### Aim

To make a radio programme suitable for a chosen audience.

### Tasks

- Continue to use the **My action planning sheet** to help you plan your work. Keep a **journal** of your group's activities to show the things you did and the problems you had.

- **Listen** to some different radio programmes.

- **Discuss** the programmes with other people.

- Decide what type of programme you will make.

- **Research** how radio programmes are made.

- Prepare a **radio script** for your programme.

- Practise reading your script.

- **Record** your programme.

- Present your programme to your chosen audience.

- **Write an evaluation report** on your programme. Use the **Report guide** to help you.

## Extension work

- Invite speakers into school to explain how radio programmes are made.

- Arrange a visit to a studio to record your radio programme.

# Planning guidelines

## What to do

1. Read the task sheets carefully and then make up your action plan of tasks to do and when to do them by completing the 'My action planning sheet'.

2. After you have completed the challenges on 'Task sheet 1', carry out the speaking and listening activities on 'Task sheet 2' so that you can analyse what a radio programme is like.

3. Begin your research into how to make a radio programme. Where can you find the information you need? Use the 'Resources' sheet to help you.

4. Prepare your script. Think about the opening of the programme, the main content and how you will end the programme.

5. Timing, sound effects, jingles and advertising are some factors to consider. Are there any others?

6. Write and practise your script. Do not be afraid to edit and change your ideas.

7. Record your programme. Note what you will need and where you can record your programme without noise or interruptions. Keep to the time limit you have allowed for the length of the programme.

8. Play your programme to the audience it is aimed at and make a note of their reactions.

9. Write a report that explains:

   a) what you have learned about radio programmes;

   b) what type of programme yours was;

   c) how the audience responded to it;

   d) how you could improve and develop your programme.

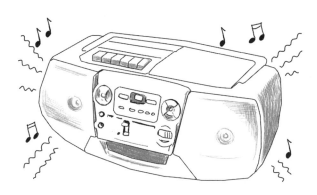

# Resources

| | | |
|---|---|---|
| **Internet** | *www.bbc.co.uk/radio4/arts*<br>This site includes various book programmes such as:<br>    Book at Bedtime<br>    Book Club<br>    Books on 4<br>    Classic Serial<br>    Book of the Week<br><br>*www.bbc.co.uk/arts/books/club/harrypotter*<br>This site shows how *Harry Potter and the Philosopher's Stone* was reviewed. | Contact the editors by email, letter or telephone. |
| **Speakers and other sources** | Invite programme makers and DJs from your local radio stations to talk to you about making programmes. | Contact your local radio stations. |
| **Libraries** | Research the reference section of the library to find information about how radio programmes are made.<br>Libraries can lend sound effect tapes/CDs. | Ask the librarian to help you. |
| **Visits** | Arrange a visit to your local radio station to see a programme being made and broadcast. Remember to ask about the technical department and how to record your programme! | Contact the station and speak to their education officer. |
| **Audience** | Select your audience and find out what they like. | Make up and carry out a survey. |
| **Your own ideas** | What else can you think of that might help you? Check your 'Planning guidelines' sheet. | Discuss your ideas with someone else. |

# Text map

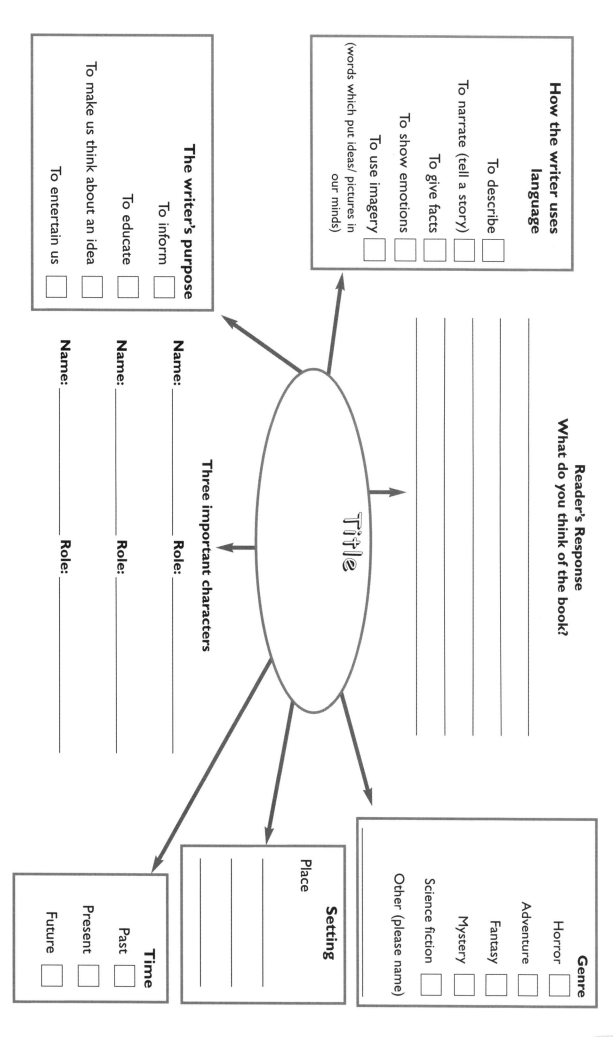

## How the writer uses language

- To describe ☐
- To narrate (tell a story) ☐
- To give facts ☐
- To show emotions ☐
- To use imagery ☐
  (words which put ideas/ pictures in our minds)

## The writer's purpose

- To inform ☐
- To educate ☐
- To make us think about an idea ☐
- To entertain us ☐

## Three important characters

Name: _____
Role: _____

Name: _____
Role: _____

Name: _____
Role: _____

**Title**

## Reader's Response
### What do you think of the book?

_____
_____
_____
_____
_____

## Genre

- Horror ☐
- Adventure ☐
- Fantasy ☐
- Mystery ☐
- Science fiction ☐
- Other (please name) ☐
  _____

## Setting

Place
_____
_____
_____

## Time

- Past ☐
- Present ☐
- Future ☐

# Character map

**How the writer uses language to present the character to the reader**

To describe the character ☐

To help develop the plot ☐

To give facts ☐

To show emotions ☐

To use imagery (words that put ideas/pictures in our minds) ☐

**The writer's purpose**

To inform about the character ☐

To show us how other characters respond to the character ☐

To make us think about the character ☐

**Reader's response**
**What do you think of this character?**

_____

_____

_____

_____

_____

**Character**

Name: _____

What do they do? _____

Why do they do it? _____

**Their role in the text**
(the part a character plays in a story)

Name: _____  Role: _____

_____

_____

_____

Name
Age
Male/Female

**Personality – the character could be:**

Outgoing          Selfish
Kind              Good tempered
Bad tempered      Stubborn
Caring            Friendly
Trustworthy       Honest
Sly

Find a page reference with an example of the characteristic.

_____

_____

_____

**Time character is in**

Past ☐

Present ☐

Future ☐

# Radio Alpha

## Features of a report
- past tense
- third person
- spelling, punctuation and grammar is accurate
- formal language
- includes facts

## Writer's purpose
- To give correct information.
- To help the reader understand how the programme is made.
- To what changes would make it better.

## Things to think about
Readers' responses.
What sense will the reader make of your report?

**My report**

## A report gives the reader information about something.
You are going to write a report to evaluate your radio programme.

## Introduction
The introduction should say what the report is going to be about. Explain what the purpose of the report is.

## Development
After the introduction write about:
- what you have learned about radio programmes;
- how the programme was planned;
- what type of programme it was;
- how the audience responded to it.

## Conclusion
First, tell your reader how you felt the programme went. Then say what sorts of things you could do to develop and improve your programme.

# Challenge 2

# Children in literature

## Teacher's notes

### Purposes

- To encourage pupils to read texts that will develop their ability to analyse the written word and identify features in texts.

- To compare texts of a similar genre that were written at different periods of time.

- To discuss issues that relate to the difficulties children face in their everyday lives.

- To develop thinking, planning and time management skills.

### Aims

- To compare the way writers have presented the plight of children in texts written in different periods.

- To produce a leaflet on the ways in which children can be helped today if they face difficulties in their lives.

### Resources required

The pupil will need copies of the following:

| | | |
|---|---|---|
| 1 | 'Challenge' sheet | page 112 |
| 2 | 'My action planning sheet' | page 113 |
| 3 | 'Task sheets' | pages 19 and 20 |
| 4 | 'Planning guidelines' | page 21 |
| 5 | 'Resources' sheet | page 22 |
| 6 | 'Text map' | page 23 |
| 7 | 'Character map' | page 24 |
| 8 | 'Compare and contrast' sheet | page 25 |
| 9 | 'Leaflet guide' | page 26 |
| 10 | Text extracts | pages 27–29 |
| 11 | 'Skills sheets' | page 114–117 |

### The teacher's role

#### 1  Introducing the challenge

Write the following in the top box of a copy of the 'Challenge sheet' (page 112):

*You are going to compare and contrast some different texts that have been written at different periods in history. They are all about children and how they are treated. You will present your findings in a report for your teacher. You are then going to find out about the difficulties children face in their lives both in the past and today.*

*Using this information you are going to design and produce a leaflet that will give guidance to modern day children who are in need of help and support in their lives.*

Then photocopy the 'Challenge sheet' and give it to the pupils. Alternatively, they could be given a blank copy of the sheet and write the challenge on it themselves. It is important for them to have the challenge to refer to.

#### 2  Providing support for the task sheets

**Reading the text extracts**

Tell the pupils that there are three extracts from the 1800s (two different ones from Charles Dickens' *Nicholas Nickleby* and one from Thomas Hughes' *Tom Brown's Schooldays*) and two from the 1900s (one from *Angela's Ashes* by Frank McCourt and one from *The Tulip Touch* by Anne Fine). Act as a guide in the discussions of the texts to help the pupils determine the issues faced by the children in the story extracts. Understanding the social/historical background of these texts will help them to appreciate the issues that are raised and enable them to carry out their tasks successfully. The teacher has the opportunity to use the extracts to further develop the pupils' understanding of issues that affect their lives or the lives of others. For example, the realisation that many children were often treated badly in the past will help them towards an investigation of how children are treated today. This will inform their decisions on what aspects of children's lives to address in their leaflet.

**Using the 'Text map'**

The 'Text map' is a means of guiding pupils through the texts and extracting accurate information from them. The map encourages discussion based on the texts and helps the pupils to form opinions about the writer's purpose. Guide the discussion so the pupils see that although the places and times are different, the texts are about similar issues.

**Using the 'Character map'**

This sheet helps the pupils to explore the characters in more depth. It allows them to identify aspects of the way in which the character is presented to the reader.

Make sure the pupil understands the purpose of the sheet and how it helps them understand the plight of the children in the stories.

**Using the 'Compare and contrast' sheet**

Completing this sheet will enable the pupil to identify elements in the texts that relate to the tasks they will be carrying out. Introduce the sheet to the pupils and discuss the meaning of the writer's purpose through the questions set on the sheet. The use of language can also be discussed to clarify any points about first or third person or tense.

**Using the 'Leaflet guide'**

This sheet will be a useful guide to the pupils when planning their leaflet. It outlines all the things that need to be taken into consideration and reminds the pupils of the purpose of the writing.

Provide the pupils with a selection of leaflets for them to discuss and evaluate so that they could list the features of a 'good' leaflet and incorporate these features into their own design. Discuss the type of language used in leaflets and how a good layout can influence the reader positively.

### 3 Other points to note

Author dates:

| | |
|---|---|
| Charles Dickens | 1812 – 1870 |
| Thomas Hughes | 1822 – 1896 |
| Frank McCourt | 1931 – |
| Anne Fine | 1947 – |

## Links to the National Curriculum

**English – Speaking and Listening**

*Level 5: In discussion, pupils pay close attention to what others say, ask questions to develop ideas and make contributions that take account of others' views. They begin to use standard English in formal situations.*

*Level 6: Pupils' talk engages the interest of the listener through the variety of vocabulary and expression.*

**English – Reading**

*Level 5: Pupils show understanding of a range of texts … identify key features, themes and characters and select sentences, phrases and relevant information to support their views.*

*Level 6: Pupils identify different layers of meaning … give personal responses to texts … summarise a range of different information from different sources.*

**English – Writing**

*Level 5: Pupils convey meaning clearly using a more formal style where appropriate.*

*Level 6: Pupils engage the reader's interest, use a range of sentence structures, use punctuation correctly to clarify meaning and ideas are organised into paragraphs.*

**PSHE and Citizenship KS2**

*2f – Pupils reflect on different social issues, using their imagination to understand other people's experiences.*

*4b – Pupils think about the lives of people living in other times.*

*4g – Pupils learn where individuals, families and groups can get help and support.*

## Links to Literacy Framework

**Year 6, Term 1**

**Word level work**

*W3 – to use dictionaries and spellchecks to clarify meaning and spelling of new words.*

*W7 – to understand how words and expressions have changed over time.*

**Sentence level work**

*S1 – to adapt texts for particular purposes.*

*S4 – to investigate the construction of sentences and identify connecting words and phrases.*

*Pupils should also begin to understand how clauses can be manipulated to achieve different effects.*

**Text level work**

*T2 – to compare and evaluate texts taking into account the viewpoint of an author.*

*T8 – to summarise a passage and compose accounts based on research.*

*Pupils should also be able to describe how texts relate to one another through themes and issues that the writer raises. They should identify features of language and use of person and discuss their effectiveness. When writing they should be able to make sustained use of the passive voice, and use paragraphs and language appropriate for the intended audience.*

# Assessment sheet

Children in literature

Name: _____ Date: _____

| | Achieved | To achieve |
|---|---|---|

## Speaking and Listening:

**Level 5:**

- Pays close attention to what people say.
- Develops ideas that are discussed.
- Contributions take into account others' views.

**Level 6:**

- Engages the interest of the listener.
- Uses appropriate vocabulary and expression.
- Is fluent in his or her use of standard English in formal situations.

## Reading:

**Level 5:**

- Understands a range of texts.
- Identifies key features, themes and characters in the text.
- Uses relevant information to support his/her views.

**Level 6:**

- Identifies layers of meaning in the chosen text.
- Gives a personal response to the text.
- Uses language and themes to develop his/her ideas about the writer's purpose.
- Understands how the writer's use of language can show how the meanings of words change over time.

## Writing:

**Level 5:**

- Writing conveys meaning clearly.
- Writing is appropriate to the task set.
- Vocabulary is used appropriately.
- Sentences are organised into paragraphs.
- Punctuation includes commas and apostrophes.
- Handwriting is joined, clear and fluent.

**Level 6:**

- Writing engages and sustains the reader's interest.
- Ideas are organised into paragraphs.
- Punctuation is used to clarify meaning.
- Handwriting is neat and legible.

# Task sheet 1

## Comparing texts

### Aim

To compare the way writers have presented the plight of children in texts written in different periods of time and present your findings in a report to your teacher.

### Tasks

• Use the **My action planning sheet** to help you plan your work.

• Read the **text extracts** and **choose two** that interest you. One must be a nineteenth century extract and the other a twentieth century extract.

• Map out the extracts using the **Text map sheet**.

• If there are characters in the extract, use the **Character map sheet** to help you work out what the characters appear to be like.

• Complete the **Compare and contrast sheet** to compare the extracts.

   What do they have in common?

   What is different?

   List the similarities and differences in the children's living conditions.

• Present a **report** to your teacher on the difficulties the children in the texts face. Your teacher will tell you whether you should write or tell this report.

# Task sheet 2

## Producing a leaflet

**Aim**

To produce a leaflet on the ways in which children can be helped today if they face difficulties in their lives.

**Tasks**

- Continue to use the **My action planning sheet** to help you plan your work.

- Find out about the living conditions of children today and the agencies that can help them.

- Use your research on children's lives today and the report you did for your teacher on children's lives in the past to help you **write up your research** under the title 'Life then and now for children'.

- **Design a leaflet** that will give guidance to children today who need help and support in their lives. Use the **Leaflet guide** to help you.

- Produce your leaflet **using a suitable computer program**. Think about how you will present it using graphics and text.

## Extension work

- Present and explain your leaflet to a social worker you have invited into school.
- Discuss with them the ways in which children who need support can be helped.

# Planning guidelines

## What to do

1. Read the task sheets carefully, then make up your action plan of tasks to do and when to do them by completing the 'My action planning sheet'. Identify the skills you will demonstrate when carrying out the tasks. Are there any skills you need help with?

2. Analyse the extracts. As you read, make notes about what you are finding out. Make sure the information will help you with your report.

3. Begin your research on children's difficulties in the past. Where can you find the information you need? History texts may help you. Use the 'Resources' sheet to help you.

4. Prepare your report. Think about:

    a) the opening;

    b) the main content – what to include;

    c) your conclusion – was life difficult for the children in the texts?

5. Write up your research. Do not be afraid to edit and change your ideas.

6. Now research the difficulties children might face in their lives today. What organisations are there to help them?

7. Design your leaflet. Think about:

    a) which aspect of children's needs today it will give advice on;

    b) the layout – headings, text boxes;

    c) graphics you will use;

    d) the computer program you will use to produce the leaflet. Will *Word Publisher* be suitable?

    Remember – the language you use should be appropriate for the audience it is aimed at.

# Resources

| | | |
|---|---|---|
| **Internet** | www.educate.org.uk/teacher_zone/classroom/ history/homes/index_poor.htm<br><br>www.childline.org.uk<br><br>www.nspcc.org.uk<br><br>www.barnados.org.uk/resources/student/history | Contact the editors by email, in writing or by telephone. |
| **Speakers and other sources** | There may be a local history group. Ask at your local museum.<br><br>Contact the Charles Dickens Museum in Portsmouth for information about Dickens. Portsmouth City Museum and Records Office, Museum Road, Portsmouth, PO1 2CT.<br><br>Rugby School may be able to provide you with information about education in Tom Brown's day. | Contact your local group and other sources. |
| **Libraries** | Social workers can give you information about how modern day children are helped.<br><br>Look in the reference section for information. | Ask the librarian to help you. |
| **Visits** | Find out if your local museum has information that will help you research the background to the novels. | Contact the museum and speak to their education officer. |
| **Audience** | Select your audience and find out what sort of information they would like in the leaflet. | Make up and carry out a survey. |
| **Your own ideas** | What else can you think of which might help you? Check your 'Planning guidelines' sheet. | Discuss your ideas with someone else. |

# Text map

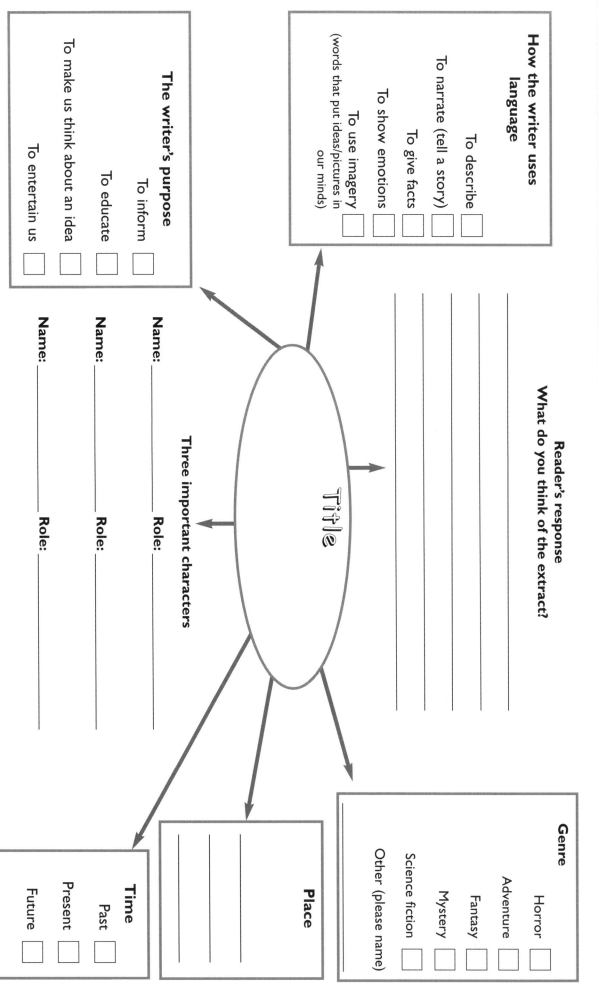

**How the writer uses language**
- To describe ☐
- To narrate (tell a story) ☐
- To give facts ☐
- To show emotions ☐
- To use imagery (words that put ideas/pictures in our minds) ☐

**The writer's purpose**
- To inform ☐
- To educate ☐
- To make us think about an idea ☐
- To entertain us ☐

**Three important characters**

Name: _____ Role: _____

Name: _____ Role: _____

Name: _____ Role: _____

Title

**Reader's response**
**What do you think of the extract?**
_____
_____
_____

**Genre**
- Horror ☐
- Adventure ☐
- Fantasy ☐
- Mystery ☐
- Science fiction ☐
- Other (please name) ☐

**Place**
_____
_____
_____

**Time**
- Past ☐
- Present ☐
- Future ☐

# Character map

**How the writer uses language to present the character to the reader**

To describe the character ☐

To help develop the plot ☐

To give facts ☐

To show emotions ☐

To use imagery (words that put ideas/pictures in our minds) ☐

**Reader's Response**
**What do you think of this character?**

_____
_____
_____
_____
_____

**The writer's purpose**

To inform about the character ☐

To show us how other characters respond to this character ☐

To make us think about the character ☐

## Character

Name: _____

What do they do? _____

Why do they do it? _____

**Their role in the text**
(what a character does in a story)

Name: _____  Role: _____

Name
Age
Male/Female

**Personality - the character could be:**

Outgoing          Selfish
Kind              Good tempered
Bad tempered      Stubborn
Caring            Friendly
Trustworthy       Honest
Sly

Find an example of the characteristic

_____
_____
_____

**Time character is in**

Past ☐

Present ☐

Future ☐

# Compare and contrast

Children in literature

| Title of text 1 | Answer these questions for each text extract | Title of text 2 |
| --- | --- | --- |
| **Writer's purpose** | **Writer's purpose**<br>What is the text about?<br><br>How do you think the writer wants the reader to respond to the text?<br><br>Identify what is the same and what is different about the writer's purpose for the two texts.<br><br>Is he or she informing, explaining or describing? | **Writer's purpose** |
| **Use of language** | **Use of language**<br>How is the language used – to retell events, to inform or to describe?<br><br>Are the sentences simple or complex?<br><br>What tense is the text written in?<br><br>Is the text in the 1st or 3rd person?<br><br>What words are used in the text that relate to time and give us an idea of the order of events? | **Use of language** |

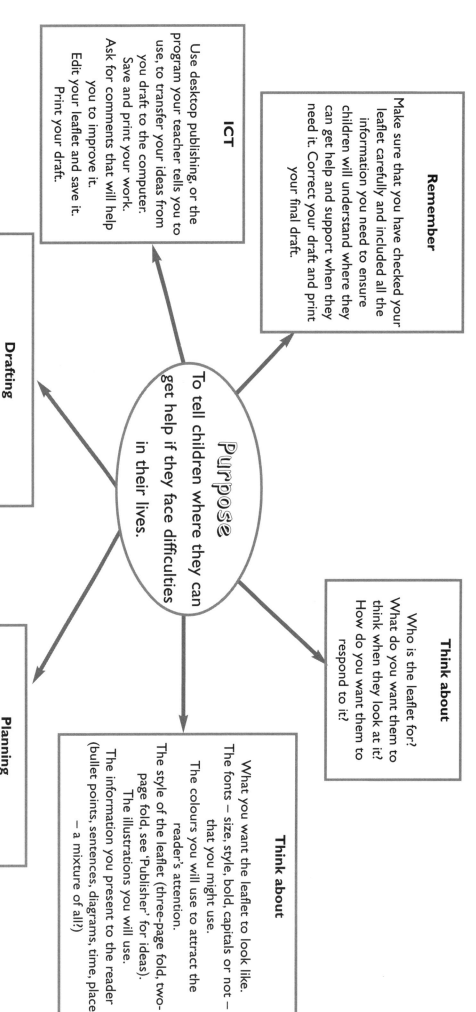

**Remember**

Make sure that you have checked your leaflet carefully and included all the information you need to ensure children will understand where they can get help and support when they need it. Correct your draft and print your final draft.

**ICT**

Use desktop publishing, or the program your teacher tells you to use, to transfer your ideas from you draft to the computer.
Save and print your work.
Ask for comments that will help you to improve it.
Edit your leaflet and save it.
Print your draft.

**Drafting**

Draw and write a clear draft of your leaflet.
Discuss it with your teacher and friends.
Is all your information correct?
Is you leaflet eye-catching?
Edit and correct your draft.

**Purpose**
To tell children where they can get help if they face difficulties in their lives.

**Think about**

Who is the leaflet for?
What do you want them to think when they look at it?
How do you want them to respond to it?

**Planning**

Draw your layout on paper.
Write out the information you will put on the leaflet.
Think about what you want to tell children and how they can be helped.

**Think about**

What you want the leaflet to look like.
The fonts – size, style, bold, capitals or not – that you might use.
The colours you will use to attract the reader's attention.
The style of the leaflet (three-page fold, two-page fold, see 'Publisher' for ideas).
The illustrations you will use.
The information you present to the reader (bullet points, sentences, diagrams, time, place – a mixture of all?)

# Text extract

**from *Nicholas Nickleby* by Charles Dickens (extract 1)**

But the pupils – the young noblemen! How the last faint traces of hope, the remotest glimmering of any good to be derived from his efforts in this den, faded from the mind of Nicholas as he looked in dismay around! Pale and haggard faces, lank and bony figures, children with the countenances of old men, deformities with irons upon their limbs, boys of stunted growth, and others whose long meagre legs would hardly bear their stooping bodies, all crowded on the view together; there were the bleared eye, the hare-lip, the crooked foot, and every ugliness or distortion that told of unnatural aversion conceived by parents for their offspring, or of young lives which, from the earliest dawn of infancy, had been one horrible endurance of cruelty and neglect. There were little faces which should have been handsome, darkened with the scowl of sullen, dogged suffering; there was childhood with the light of its eye quenched, its beauty gone, and its helplessness alone remaining; there were vicious-faced boys, brooding, with leaden eyes, like malefactors in a jail; and there were young creatures on whom the sins of their frail parents had descended, weeping even for the mercenary nurses they had known, and lonesome even in their loneliness. With every kindly sympathy and affection blasted in its birth, with every young and healthy feeling flogged and starved down, with every revengeful passion that can fester in swollen hearts eating its evil way to their core in silence, what an incipient Hell was breeding here!

**from *Nicholas Nickleby* by Charles Dickens (extract 2)**

It induced him to consider the boy more attentively, and he was surprised to observe the extraordinary mixture of garments which formed his dress. Although he could not have been less than eighteen or nineteen years old, and was tall for that age, he wore a skeleton suit, such as is usually put upon very little boys, and which, though most absurdly short in the arms and legs, was quite wide enough for his attenuated frame. In order that the lower part of his legs might be in perfect keeping with this singular dress, he had a very large pair of boots, originally made for tops, which might have been once worn by some stout farmer, but were now too patched and tattered for a beggar.

Heaven knows how long he had been there, but he still wore the same linen which he had first taken down; for, round his neck, was a tattered child's frill, only half concealed by a coarse, man's neckerchief. He was lame; and as he feigned to be busy in arranging the table, glanced at the letters with a look so keen, and yet so dispirited and hopeless, that Nicholas could hardly bear to watch him.

'What are you bothering about there, Smike?' cried Mrs. Squeers; 'let the things alone, can't you?'

'Eh!' said Squeers, looking up. 'Oh! it's you, is it?'

'Yes, sir,' replied the youth, pressing his hands together, as though to control, by force, the nervous wandering of his fingers; 'Is there –'

'Well!' said Squeers.

'Have you – did anybody – has nothing been heard – about me?'

'Devil a bit,' replied Squeers testily.

The lad withdrew his eyes, and, putting his hand to his face, moved towards the door.

'Not a word,' resumed Squeers, 'and never will be. Now, this is a pretty sort of thing, isn't it, that you should have been left here, all these years, and no money paid after the first six – nor no notice taken, nor no clue to be got who you belong to? It's a pretty sort of thing that I should have to feed a great fellow like you, and never hope to get one penny for it, isn't it?'

The boy put his hand to his head as if he were making an effort to recollect something, and then, looking vacantly at his questioner, gradually broke into a smile, and limped away.

# Text extract

## from *Tom Brown's Schooldays* by Thomas Hughes

The lower-fourth form, in which Tom found himself at the beginning of the next half-year, was the largest form in the lower school, and numbered upwards of forty boys. Young gentlemen of all ages, from nine to fifteen, were to be found there, who expended such part of their energies as was devoted to Latin and Greek upon a book of Livy, the Bucolics of Virgil, and the Hecuba of Euripides, which were ground out in small daily portions. The driving of this unlucky lower-fourth must have been grievous work to the unfortunate master, for it was the most unhappily constituted of any in the school. Here stuck the great stupid boys, who for the life of them could never master the accidence; the objects alternatively of mirth and terror to the youngsters, who were daily taking them up and laughing at them in lesson, and getting kicked by them for so doing in play-hours…

…Then came the mass of the form, boys of eleven and twelve, the most mischievous and reckless age of British youth, of whom East and Tom Brown were fair specimens. As full of tricks as monkeys, and of excuses as Irish women, making fun of their master, one another, and their lessons, Argus himself would have been puzzled to keep an eye on them; and as for making them steady or serious for half-an-hour together, it was simply hopeless. The remainder of the form consisted of young prodigies of nine and ten, who were going up the school at the rate of a form a half-year, all boys' hands and wits being against them in their progress. It would have been one man's work to see that the precocious youngsters had fair play; and as the master had a great deal besides to do, they hadn't, and were for ever being shoved down three or four places, their verses stolen, their books inked, their jackets whitened, and their lives otherwise made a burden to them…

…Tom, as has been said, had come up from the third with a good character, but the temptations of the lower-fourth soon proved too strong for him, and he rapidly fell away; and became as unmanageable as the rest.

### from *Angela's Ashes* by Frank McCourt

...There are six or seven barefoot boys in my class and they don't say anything and I wonder if it's better to have shoes with rubber tires that make you trip and stumble or to go barefoot. If you have no shoes at all you'll have all the barefoot boys on your side. If you have rubber tires on your shoes you're all alone with your brother and you have to fight your own battles. I sit on a bench in the schoolyard shed and take off my shoes and stockings but when I go into the class the master wants to know where my shoes are. He knows I'm not one of the barefoot boys and he makes me go back into the yard, bring in the shoes and put them on. Then he says to the class, There is sneering here. There is jeering at the misfortune of others. Is there anyone in this class that thinks he's perfect? Raise your hands.

There are no hands.

Is there anyone in this class that comes from a rich family with money galore to spend on shoes? Raise your hands.

There are no hands.

He says, There are boys who have to mend their shoes whatever way they can. There are boys in this class with no shoes at all. It's not their fault and it's no shame. Our Lord had no shoes. He died shoeless. Do you see Him hanging on the cross sporting shoes? Do you boys?

No, sir.

What is it you don't see Our Lord doing?

Hanging on the cross and sporting shoes, sir.

Now if I hear of one boy in this class jeering and sneering at McCourt or his brother over their shoes the stick will come out. What will come out, boys?

The stick, sir.

The stick will sting, boys. The ash plant will whistle through the air, it will land on the backside of the boy that jeers, the boy that sneers. Where will it land, boys?

On the boy that jeers, sir.

And?

The boy that sneers, sir.

The boys bother us no more and we wear our shoes with the rubber tires the few weeks to Easter when the St. Vincent de Paul Society gives us the gift of boots.

# Text extract

### from *The Tulip Touch* by Anne Fine

I hated Tulip's house. It wasn't just that the carpets were stained and the furniture battered. It was that Tulip herself seemed different, just a shell. As if she had slipped away invisibly and left some strange, strained imitation in her place to say to me, 'What shall we do now?' or 'Want another biscuit?'

I pushed the packet of damp crumbs aside. I'd have suggested going into her bedroom, but the glimpse of a stained sheet spread over a chair to dry as she kicked the door closed had warned me that wouldn't be welcome.

'Shall we go in the yard?'

I wanted to get out of the kitchen. Tulip's mother was giving me the creeps with her beg-pardon smile and her tireless, tuneless humming; as if, in that horrible, smelly, sunless back room, she'd completely forgotten a song was supposed to have a melody, let alone a beginning and an ending. Hearing that awful, interminable drone was like listening to a robot pretend to be a person.

The backyard had clumps of weeds waist high. But there were far too many smashed bottles lying about for us to play most of our creeping games. So, in desperation I said:

'Let's go and find your kitten.'

She looked at me blankly.

'Well,' I corrected myself, feeling stupid. 'Cat, by now.'

'We don't have a cat.'

'You were carrying one the day I met you.'

Her eyes went pebble hard.

'I expect I had to give it away.'

I knew she was lying. So, in my eyes, of course, it was a merciless cat killer I met when, retreating from the unpromising yard, we came face to face with Mr. Pierce, striding in through another door. I watched as he filled a cracked cup with water, drank it down, refilled it, drank more, then turned back from the sink. His eyes came to rest on me, and never moved till I snatched up my jacket and, burbling excuses, rushed away.

# Challenge 3

# Historical texts

## Teacher's notes

### Purposes

- To help pupils apply their understanding and use of non-fiction texts as a means of developing their understanding of a fiction text.

- To compare texts that are written in different periods of time about different issues.

- To identify time and place in a text through the use of language.

- To develop thinking, planning and time management skills.

### Aims

- To identify the time and place of an historical text through the use of language.

- To write a short story using information gained from historical research to develop a realistic background and setting for the story.

### Resources required

The pupil will need copies of the following:

| | | |
|---|---|---|
| 1 | 'Challenge sheet' | page 112 |
| 2 | 'My action planning sheet' | page 113 |
| 3 | 'Task sheets' | pages 35 and 36 |
| 4 | 'Planning guidelines' | page 37 |
| 5 | 'Resources' sheet | page 38 |
| 6 | 'Text map' | page 39 |
| 7 | 'Story guide' | page 40 |
| 8 | Text extracts | pages 41 and 42 |
| 9 | 'Skills sheets' | page 114–117 |

### The teacher's role

#### 1 Introducing the challenge

Write the following in the top box of a copy of the 'Challenge sheet' (page 112):

*You are going to explore the background and setting of an historical text using either the text extracts provided or a text of your own choice.*

*You are then going to find out about the period that the text was written in and use this research to help you*

*develop a realistic background and setting for a short story that you are going to write.*

Then photocopy the 'Challenge sheet' and give it to the pupils. Alternatively, they could be given a blank copy of the sheet and write the challenge on it themselves. It is important for them to have the challenge to refer to.

#### 2 Providing support for the tasks sheets

**Reading the text extracts**

Sharing the texts could be carried out as a whole class activity with the teacher acting as a guide in the discussion of them. He or she could then work with part of the class to help them complete the 'Text Map' together while the more able pupils work independently.

The extracts provide opportunities to explore historical writing that is set in different times and that raises different issues – the morality of slavery (*Chains*) and the difficulties of living through a war (*Blitzcat*). They also provide an opportunity for the pupils to identify clues to the time and place of a story through the language used in the text. Direct the pupils' attention to words and phrases that show that the text is not set in modern times. Sharing books about slavery and/or World War II will help identify common features of the particular time period.

After discussing the texts, help the pupils select which one they are going to use as a basis for their research (or help them choose a different text altogether).

**Using the 'Text map'**

The 'Text map' is a means of guiding pupils through the texts and extracting accurate information from them. It encourages discussion based on the texts and helps the pupils form an opinion about the writer's purpose. The map is a means of showing the pupils the elements that make up a text in terms of background – the place and the time. Teacher-led discussion will help the pupils realise the importance of context in a text. The reader is more able to make sense of the text if he or she understands the reason why the background and setting are appropriate for the narrative.

The boxes on the sheet can be used to record a page reference number where appropriate.

**Using the 'Story guide'**

This sheet helps the pupils plan their ideas within a writing framework that guides but does not dictate their planning.

# Challenge 3 continued

Help the pupils realise that their story has different elements:

- the introduction may set the scene and introduce the characters;
- the development of the story needs to ensure that the reader finds the background and setting believable. The behaviour of the characters should be in keeping with the time period described in the narrative;
- the conclusion should draw the narrative threads together and leave the reader feeling that a good tale has been told.

Discuss drafting, editing and redrafting as a positive way of developing ideas in an extended story. Pupils should be able to sustain a narrative and write using appropriate language, spelling and grammar.

## Links to the National Curriculum

**English – Speaking and Listening**

*Level 5: Pupils talk confidently using appropriate language and develop their ideas.*
*Level 6: Pupils adapt their talk to a formal context and engage the interest of the listener.*

**English – Reading**

*Level 5: Pupils select essential points from a range of texts. They retrieve and collate information.*
*Level 6: Pupils identify different layers of meaning and summarise a range of information from different sources.*

**English – Writing**

*Level 5: Vocabulary choices are appropriate and imaginative. Writing is set out in paragraphs and punctuation is generally accurate.*
*Level 6: Writing sustains the reader's interest and sentence structures and vocabulary are used to create the desired effects. Punctuation is used to clarify meaning and writing is organised into paragraphs.*

**History**

*Level 5: Pupils can identify features of past societies and make links with them. They evaluate sources of information and identify those that are useful for particular tasks.*
*Level 6: Pupils use their factual knowledge to describe past societies and periods. They identify and analyse interpretations of events. They identify and evaluate sources of information which they use to produce structured work.*

## Links to Literacy Framework

**Year 6, Term 2**

**Word level work**
*W3 – to use dictionaries and spellchecks to clarify meaning and spelling of new words.*

**Sentence level work**
*S1 – to adapt texts for particular purposes. (Revision of Term 1.)*

**Text level work**
*T12 – to write an extended story, worked on over time with a theme identified in reading.*

# Assessment sheet

Name: _____  Date: _____

| | Achieved | To achieve |
|---|---|---|
| **Speaking and Listening:** | | |
| **Level 5:** | | |
| • Talks confidently using appropriate language. | | |
| • Develops ideas that are discussed. | | |
| **Level 6:** | | |
| • Adapts talk to a formal context. | | |
| • Engages the interest of the listener. | | |
| **Reading:** | | |
| **Level 5:** | | |
| • Selects essential points from a range of texts. | | |
| • Retrieves and collates information. | | |
| **Level 6:** | | |
| • Identifies layers of meaning in the chosen text. | | |
| • Summarises information from different sources. | | |
| **Writing:** | | |
| **Level 5:** | | |
| • Vocabulary choices are appropriate and imaginative. | | |
| • Writing is in paragraphs and punctuation is generally accurate. | | |
| **Level 6:** | | |
| • Writing engages and sustains the reader's interest. | | |
| • Sentence structures and vocabulary are used to create the desired effects. | | |
| • Punctuation is used to clarify meaning and writing is organised into paragraphs. | | |
| **History:** | | |
| **Level 5:** | | |
| • Features of past societies are identified and links made with them. | | |
| • Sources of information are used and identified. | | |
| **Level 6:** | | |
| • Factual knowledge is used to describe past societies. | | |
| • Identifies and analyses interpretations of events. | | |
| • Identifies sources to produce structured work. | | |

# Task sheet 1

## Exploring the setting of an historical text

### Aim

To identify the time and place of an historical text through the use of language.

### Tasks

- Use the **My action planning sheet** to help you plan your work.

- Select a **text extract** from those provided or choose your own text. Read it carefully.

- **Write** down a few sentences that will help to remind you what it is about.

- Map out the extract using the **Text map sheet** as a guide. In particular:
    - list the words that give you ideas about when the story is set;
    - list the clues from the text that tell you **when** the story is set.

- **Write** down your own ideas about the background and setting of the text. Think about the following:
    - the clues the writer gives you in the text;
    - the words used – are they modern, old fashioned, from a different time period?

- List the words that give you ideas about **where** the story is set.

- What do you know about this period?

- **Explain** to others in your group why you think the writer has set the story in this background and setting.

# Task sheet 2

## Writing a short story

### Aim

To write a short story using the information gained from historical research to develop a realistic background and setting for your story.

### Tasks

- Continue to use the **My action planning sheet** to help you plan your work.

- **Find out** more about the historical period in which your chosen text extract is written. Use non-fiction information books, CD-Roms and the internet to help you. Write a bibliography of your sources.

- Use these resources to check that the writer of your chosen text extract is accurate in his or her descriptions of the history, lifestyle or science of the time which the text describes.

- **Choose** a suitable background and setting for your story. Invent some appropriate characters who will fit this setting.

- **Write a detailed story** centred around these characters and what happens to them. Use the **Story guide** to help you. Make sure your story includes appropriate words that would be used during this time period.

- **Share** your story with someone else. Then edit it and produce a final draft.

## Extension work

- To develop your story visually, make a collage that shows what people looked like and the clothes they wore.

- Find out about the type of music they would have listened to.

# Planning guidelines

## What to do

1. Read the task sheets carefully and then prepare your action plan of tasks to do and when to do them by completing the 'My action planning sheet'. Identify the skills you will demonstrate when carrying out the tasks. Are there any skills you need help with?

2. Choose one of the two text extracts to evaluate.

3. Carry out the speaking and listening tasks first so that you can analyse the extract and discuss the information found in it.

4. Begin your research. Where can you find the information you need? History texts may be useful. Use the 'Resources' sheet to help you.

5. Plan your story. Use the 'Story guide' to help you. Edit the draft, redraft and edit it again in order to improve your work. If you use a word processor, remember to save your work as you complete it. Think about how you will present your final draft.

6. Write a bibliography at the end of your story that shows your sources of information. Set it out as follows:

   last name of author or editor, their initials, title of the publication, publisher's name and date of publication.

   For example:

   Canning, J (ed), *The Illustrated Macaulay's History of England*. Guild Publishing, 1988

7. In addition to your bibliography, list the following:

   • website addresses and the date the site was used;

   • the names of people who helped you;

   • the names of places you visited and the information you obtained from these people and visits.

# Resources

| | | |
|---|---|---|
| **Internet** | General information about slavery<br>*www.spartacus.schoolnet.co.uk/USAslavery.htm*<br><br>Bristol and the slave trade<br>*www.headleypark.bristol.sch.uk/slavery/index.htm*<br><br>Slave ships<br>*www.spartacus.schoolnet.co.uk/USASships.htm* | Check 'Encarta' and similar other CD-Roms. |
| **Speakers and other sources** | Speakers from museums and history groups may be useful.<br><br>Museums may provide artefacts from the period. | The local museum may have examples of lifestyles. |
| **Libraries** | Encyclopaedias and non-fiction texts on specific subjects will help with research. | Ask the librarian to help you. |
| **Visits** | A trip to a place which has information or examples which will help your research may be useful. | Trips can be out of school activities as well as those organised by the school. |
| **Your own ideas** | Researching as many different aspects of your chosen background and setting as you can will help you develop good ideas for your writing. | Discuss your ideas with someone else. |

# Text map

## Historical texts

### How the writer uses language

To describe ☐

To narrate (tell a story) ☐

To give facts ☐

To show emotions ☐

To use imagery to place the story in a particular context ☐

### The writer's purpose

To inform ☐

To educate ☐

To make us think about the text in terms of background and setting ☐

To entertain us ☐

**Title**

### Reader's ideas

**What is the background to this text and where is it set?**

_____

_____

_____

_____

_____

### Genre

Horror ☐

Adventure ☐

Fantasy ☐

Mystery ☐

Science fiction ☐

Autobiographical/biographical ☐

Other _____ ☐

### Why this background and setting?

How does the setting of the text help the reader make sense of the information given?

How does understanding the background of the story help the reader make sense of the text?

### Place

What sort of setting does the writer place the story in?

List the words used in the text which indicate what the place might be.

List the clues which tell you where the action is taking place.

### Time

Past ☐

Present ☐

Future ☐

# Story guide

## Historical texts

### Language

Narrative — tells the story.

Descriptive — sets the scene.

Make sure the spelling and punctuation are accurate.

Remember to use dialogue — but not too much!

### Content

What is being written about?

What is the subject matter?

Introduction — try to engage the reader's interest.

Development — make a spider diagram of your ideas for the facts, ideas and narrative.

Conclusion — draw your ideas together for a satisfactory ending!

### Writer's purpose

Why are you writing?

What do you want the reader to learn?

What ideas and information do you need to include?

### Reader's response

What sense will the reader make of your story?

TITLE OF STORY

### Genre

Horror ☐

Adventure ☐

Fantasy ☐

Mystery ☐

Science fiction ☐

Autobiographical/biographical ☐

Other _____ ☐

### Research

Think about your story — what information does the reader need?

Where will you find information for your setting, background and characters?

# Text extract

## from *Blitzcat* by Robert Westall

The front lawn of Brereton House was littered with kids' tricycles, balls and tiny red sandals. Through the wide-open windows at least two babies could be heard crying. Florence Wensley answered the door. Sergeant Millom had always thought her very much a lady, but she didn't look a lady this morning. She looked a pale, weary wreck; her fair hair was greasy, hanging in strands round her face. She was holding the baby, and the baby had been a bit sick down her jumper. And when she saw Sergeant Millom's uniform she went as white as a sheet.

'Geoff,' she said. 'Something's happened to Geoff.'

Sergeant Millom remembered the husband in the RAF. Flying Blenheims somewhere in France. They said Blenheims were flying death-traps; too slow, not enough guns. They said Jerry was eating them in handfuls for breakfast. They said Geoff Wensley was the last of his old squadron still alive.

And Geoff was lost somewhere in France; like Tom. Millom wanted to say something to comfort her; to say they hadn't come about her husband. But Hillfield took his wrist in a grip like iron, and said coldly, 'Can we go inside, Mrs Wensley?'

The swine didn't care. He was using it to break her up. All he wanted was his spy. A confession.

They went into a front room; pretty once, but faded now, and littered with children's toys worse than the lawn. Florence Wensley sat down in the sagging settee like a falling brick. She was away somewhere inside herself, her eyes blank. The baby, catching her mood, began to cry. Florence's long, pale hands moved automatically to soothe it, like mechanical things. The lines seemed to grow across her face as Sergeant Millom watched. She seemed to wither, turning into an old woman. That's what will happen to me, he thought, when I hear about Tom.

Mrs Wensley made an effort. Her blue-grey eyes came back into focus, like a submarine coming up to the surface, putting up a terrified blue periscope.

'He was only twenty-five,' she said. 'The RAF was his whole life. He was a Regular. He joined up in 1938, straight from university...'

Sergeant Millom could bear it no longer. He blurted out, 'It's not about your husband, Mrs Wensley. It's about that telegram you sent.'

She stared at him, her head turning slowly. 'Not dead?' she said. 'What telegram?'

'A telegram about Lord Gort...'

She looked bewildered. 'Lord Gort? She's lost.'

Sergeant Millom thought he was going mad. 'She's lost?'

'Lord Gort's a cat... Geoff's cat. We got her when the war broke out. As a kitten. The BEF was going to France, and everyone was talking about Lord Gort. So Geoff called her Lord Gort. We thought she was a tom; but she had kittens. Mummy and I brought her here when we were evacuated from Dover, but she wouldn't settle. She went missing five days ago. We thought she'd go home to Dover. So I telegrammed our old housekeeper to keep an eye open for her... has she turned up?'

## from *Chains* by Frances Mary Hendry

'…Sceptics like the Jacobins, atheists and deists — of whom I fear Pitt is one, and also that idiot Wilberforce — denounce slavery, certainly. So do some Nonconformists; the Quakers keep no slaves, and the Methodist preacher Wesley urged his followers to free theirs, though few obeyed him — the Methodists and Baptists own thousands of blacks. But should true Christians oppose it? Neither Christ himself, nor any of the early Christian writers, ever condemned slavery. Many urge the humane treatment of slaves, certainly, but the early church leader Augustine in his famous work 'The City of God' flatly declares that slavery is the Lord's punishment for sin, and in God's eyes slave dealing is no crime.'

He considered, staring out towards the shore. 'The blacks taken as slaves seem luckless, but might well die of disease or war or be sacrificed to their heathen gods, if they were not removed from Africa. You dislike the cruelty and injustice of slavery, as all good men do; but you are predisposed to softness. You are rich, and, if you will forgive me, pampered. My mother died of starvation when I was six years old.' Juliet's jaw dropped in shock. 'Life is cruel and unfair for whites, as for blacks.'

To hide his emotion, apparently, Owens sent a glare down at the launch ferrying back the full casks. 'Mister Cartwright, I have no wish to remain here until next year!' he called, before turning back to Juliet to continue his lecture.

'You must also consider the purely practical argument. Without slavery the New World plantations and their trade in sugar, rice and tobacco, and nowadays cotton, which provide a huge part of Britain's wealth, simply could not survive. Half the small manufacturers of England, who supply goods for the trade, would be ruined. The fight against the French would collapse for lack of taxes. Thus even if the abolitionists could persuade Parliament to ban the traffic, the Africa trade must necessarily continue. No, no. Man will learn to fly before the barren places of the earth can become fertile farmland without slaves.'

He nodded seriously. 'Also, while the trade is legal, the Government may monitor it and soften its harshness, as with the bounty, and laws regulating the number of slaves that may be carried in ships of different sizes. Decent men like myself take care of our blacks, making an honest profit from a vital and respectable, if unpleasant, trade. I treat my cargo with as much care and consideration as is consistent with safety. And, of course, profit. There are far worse ships than mine. Many, I fear. Even most. However, if the trade is outlawed, its conditions can only worsen. None but rogues will take part in it, smuggling slaves, cramming in as many souls as they can without regard to their humanity.'

# Animals in literature

## Teacher's notes

### Purposes

- To understand how writers have used animals to tell stories.

- To compare how different writers present animals in their stories.

- To investigate how the personification of animals in literature has led to stereotyping which can condition our thinking about animals as they really are.

- To develop a viewpoint based on reading and research and to present this viewpoint in a discussion text.

- To develop thinking, planning and time management skills.

### Aims

- To investigate how writers present animals in stories.

- To write a discussion text that answers the question: 'Does the way animals are portrayed in stories influence the way we think about them?'

### Resources required

The pupil will need copies of the following:

| | | |
|---|---|---|
| 1 | 'Challenge sheet' | page 112 |
| 2 | 'My action planning sheet' | page 113 |
| 3 | 'Task sheets' | pages 46 and 47 |
| 4 | 'Planning guidelines' | page 48 |
| 5 | 'Resources' sheet | page 49 |
| 6 | 'Animal character map' | page 50 |
| 7 | 'Comparison sheet' | page 51 |
| 8 | 'Report guide' | page 52 |
| 9 | 'Discussion text guide' | page 53 |
| 10 | Text extracts | pages 54–57 |
| 11 | 'Skills sheets' | pages 114–117 |

### The teacher's role

#### 1 Introducing the challenge

Write the following in the top box of a copy of the 'Challenge sheet' (page 112):

*You are going to find out how writers present animals in stories and compare this with what animals are like in real life.*

*You are then going to write a discussion text that answers the following question: 'Does the way animals are presented in stories influence the way we think about them?*

Then photocopy the 'Challenge sheet' and give it to the pupils. Alternatively, they could be given a blank copy of the sheet and write the challenge on it themselves. It is important for them to have the challenge to refer to.

#### 2 Providing support for the task sheets

**Reading the text extracts**

The extracts give an insight into the character of the animals concerned as the author has presented them. Guide the discussion of the texts to help the pupils understand how the author has personified the animals in the story. How does this make us think about the animals? Does stereotyping affect the way we think about real animals?

Help the pupils compare the writing styles of the authors and their presentation of themes and issues through the animals' points of view. The pupils need to decide how the animal or human characteristics presented show how animals are used in literature.

The sharing of the texts could be carried out as a whole class with the teacher modelling how to complete an 'Animal character map sheet'. The more able pupils could then go on to give the 'Animal character map sheet' more detail before completing the 'Comparison sheet' and writing a report on the way the authors have presented the animals to the reader.

**Using the 'Animal character map'**

The 'Animal character map' guides the pupil through a deconstruction of the animal character in the story and helps examine the writer's purpose.

Lead a discussion about how the animals have been presented in the texts and discuss each question on the map sheet with the pupils and ask them to write down their responses.

**Using the 'Comparison sheet'**

The purpose of the 'Comparison sheet' is to allow each text extract to be examined in more detail. Use this sheet to help the pupils identify and collect specific words that are used and to look at the type of language and sentence structure used by each author. Explain that the author's purpose can be to tell a story or make the reader think about an idea or a situation. The sheet will help the pupils to focus on the human and animal characteristics portrayed in the extracts.

## Using the 'Report guide'

This sheet can be used to help the pupils write their report as suggested in 'Task sheet 1'. The sheet provides the pupil with a framework to develop the formal piece of writing. Discuss the sheet with the pupils to share ideas about the points made on it.

## Using the 'Discussion text guide'

This sheet enables the pupils to plan their writing in a structured way. The emphasis is on the need to decide what ideas and information should be included in order to present their point of view effectively. Direct the discussion with the pupils and guide them with the note taking that will help with the written work.

### 3   Other points to note

'Task sheet 2' requires the pupils to use the information gathered during the completion of 'Task sheet 1'. The tasks encourage the pupil to use a variety of sources in order to develop a viewpoint for their discussion text. The teacher should remind the pupils to use their previous research, maps and comparison sheet to develop their ideas and information gathering. An important skill is the ability to select essential information. The use of fact to inform and develop a viewpoint is a skill which the more able pupil should be able to demonstrate.

## Links to the National Curriculum

### English – Speaking and Listening

*Level 5: Pupils listen, ask relevant questions, respond to others. Pupils make contributions in discussion that are relevant to the topic.*
*Level 6: Pupils can summarise the main points of a discussion; they can consider the alternative viewpoints and can reach agreement. They are fluent in their use of Standard English in a formal situation.*

### English – Reading

*Level 5: Pupils can identify how characters are created. They can read for information. They can retrieve and collate information successfully.*
*Level 6: Pupils can evaluate ideas and themes, thus broadening their perspectives and extending their thinking. Pupils can summarise a range of information from different sources and use it effectively.*

### English – Writing

*Level 5: Pupils demonstrate that their writing is appropriate for the task set. They use punctuation accurately.*
*Level 6: The pupil's writing explores ideas and engages the reader's interest. An impersonal style of writing is used for the tasks set which informs and persuades the reader. Punctuation is used to clarify meaning and paragraphs are used to introduce new ideas.*

### Science

*Level 5: Pupils show an increasing knowledge and understanding of life processes and living things. Pupils select information from a range of varied sources.*
*Level 6: Pupils use knowledge and understanding to describe and explain life processes and features of living things. Pupils select and use sources of information effectively.*

## Links to Literacy Framework

### Year 6, Term 2

#### Word level work

*W8 – to build a bank of useful terms and phrases for argument; for example, similarly … whereas.*

#### Sentence level work

*S3 – to use punctuation correctly in complex sentences.*

#### Text level work

*T14 – to write commentaries or summaries crediting views expressed by using expressions such as 'The writer says that…'*
*T15 – to recognise how arguments are constructed to be effective.*
*T18 – to construct effective arguments.*

'Animals in literature' can be used to introduce the way in which writers present their ideas to the reader using a non-human voice.

# Assessment sheet

Name: _____ Date: _____

| | Achieved | To achieve |
|---|---|---|

## Speaking and Listening:

**Level 5:**
- Makes contributions relevant to the topic.
- Takes into account others' views.

**Level 6:**
- Can summarise points made and consider alternatives.
- Is fluent in use of standard English.

## Reading:

**Level 5:**
- Can identify how characters are created.
- Retrieves and collates information successfully.

**Level 6:**
- Can evaluate ideas, thus extending thinking skills.
- Can summarise a range of information from different sources.

## Writing:

**Level 5:**
- Writing is appropriate for the task set.
- Punctuation is used accurately.

**Level 6:**
- Writing explores ideas and engages the reader's interest.
- A formal, impersonal style is used for the tasks set.
- Punctuation is used to clarify meaning and writing is organised into paragraphs.

## Science:

**Level 5:**
- Shows an understanding of life processes and living things.
- Can select information from a range of varied sources.

**Level 6:**
- Uses knowledge and understanding to describe and explain life processes and features of living things.
- Selects and uses sources of information effectively.

# Task sheet 1

## Investigating a text

### Aim

To investigate how writers present animals in stories.

### Tasks

- Use the **My action planning sheet** to help you plan your work.

- **Read** each text extract at least twice.

- **Discuss** with other people in your group how the animals are presented to the reader. How do they compare with their real-life counterparts?

- Using the **Animal character map**:

  – map out the character for each animal. Note any good or bad points;

  – list the 'human' qualities the animals appear to have;

  – identify the 'real' animal characteristics the characters have, if any. You may need to research the animal to identify its real characteristics.

- Use the **Comparison sheet** to help you compare the human qualities the animals may appear to have with their animal characteristics.

- **Write** a short report on the way that the writers have presented the animals to the reader. What is your response to them? Use the **Report guide** to help you. Present this report to others in your group.

# Task sheet 2

## Writing a discussion text

### Aim

To write a discussion text to answer the following question:
'Does the way animals are presented in stories influence the way we think about them?'

### Tasks

• Continue to use the **My action planning sheet** to help you plan your work.

• **Find out** how rats and rabbits live in the wild. **Compare** this with the way the animals are presented in the text extracts. What is similar/different?

• **Decide** what you personally think about the way animals are presented in stories and how this affects the way people think about them.

• **Plan** your answer to the question using the **Discussion text guide**.

• **Write** your discussion text. Read it through carefully. Does it make sense?
Have you presented your viewpoint effectively?

• **Edit** your writing and make any changes you think necessary.

## Extension work

• Investigate how animals are portrayed in cartoons and films.
• Design and draw a comic strip about an animal character.

# Planning guidelines

## What to do

1. Read the task sheets carefully and then make up your action plan of tasks to do and when to do them by completing the 'My action planning sheet'. Identify the skills you will demonstrate when carrying out the tasks. Are there any skills you need help with?

2. Carry out the speaking and listening tasks first so that you can share your ideas about how animals are presented in stories with other people in your group.

3. When writing your report, use the 'Animal character map', 'Comparison sheet' and 'Report guide' to help you.

4. For 'Task sheet 2', carry out the research first so that you have the information you need to help you make an informed decision about the effect writers have on how we view animals.

5. Remember to keep a record of your sources of information in case you need to refer to them again.

6. Make sure you plan your writing in detail before you start it. You will need to have all the information you require before you start writing. Remember you are presenting your point of view. Think about your answer to the question before you start to plan.

7. Check your draft and edit it carefully before you produce your final piece. If you are word processing your work, think about including pictures downloaded from the computer.

8. Try to ensure that your writing presents your answer to the question in a way that will persuade the reader to agree with you.

# Resources

| | | |
|---|---|---|
| **Internet** | For research into the animals: *www.bbc.co.uk/nature/animals/pets/mice.shtml* <br><br> Information and facts: *www.bbc.co.uk/nature/wildlife/factfiles/266.shtml* (site about mice) <br><br> *www.bbc.co.uk/nature/wildlife/factfiles/198.shtml* (site about rabbits) <br><br> *www.bbc.co.uk/nature/wildlife/factfiles/272.shtml* (site about rats) <br><br> For pictures: *http://whom.co.uk/squelch/british_wildlife.htm* | Check 'Encarta' and similar other CD-Roms. |
| **Speakers and other sources** | You can invite a vet into school to talk about small mammals. <br><br> The RSPCA may have information that will help you. <br><br> Local breeders can be contacted and invited to talk about the animals they breed. | You can write or phone to invite speakers into school. |
| **Libraries** | You will find animal books in the library. Non-fiction for facts, fiction for stories. | Ask the librarian to help you. |
| **Visits** | You can visit a local wildlife sanctuary or zoo. | Trips can be out of school activities as well as those organised by the school. |
| **Audience** | You are preparing work for your class. Think about what will interest them. Do a survey on how many of them read animal stories? | |
| **Your own ideas** | Discuss your ideas with your teacher and friends. Do they have information about animals that you need? | Discuss your ideas with someone else. |

# Animal character map

## Animals in literature

### Using this page

Look at the boxes – they will help you develop your ideas and views about the animal characters in the text extracts.

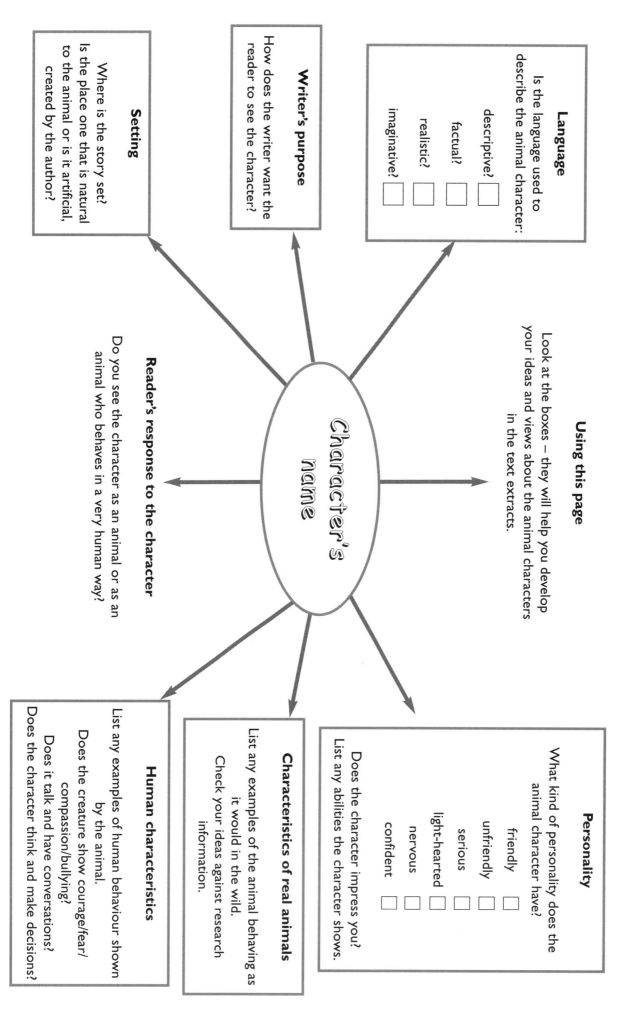

**Language**

Is the language used to describe the animal character:

descriptive? ☐

factual? ☐

realistic? ☐

imaginative? ☐

**Writer's purpose**

How does the writer want the reader to see the character?

**Setting**

Where is the story set? Is the place one that is natural to the animal or is it artificial, created by the author?

*Character's name*

**Reader's response to the character**

Do you see the character as an animal or as an animal who behaves in a very human way?

**Personality**

What kind of personality does the animal character have?

friendly ☐

unfriendly ☐

serious ☐

light-hearted ☐

nervous ☐

confident ☐

Does the character impress you? List any abilities the character shows.

**Characteristics of real animals**

List any examples of the animal behaving as it would in the wild.

Check your ideas against research information.

**Human characteristics**

List any examples of human behaviour shown by the animal.

Does the creature show courage/fear/ compassion/bullying?

Does it talk and have conversations?

Does the character think and make decisions?

# Comparison sheet

**Title of text**_____

**Name of animal character**_____

| What is the text about? | List the human qualities of this character. |
| --- | --- |
| Identify what the writer is showing the reader about the character. | List the animal qualities of this character. |
| How is language used to describe the character and the situation? | List words that help the reader understand the animal's characteristics. |
| Are the sentences simple or complex? | |
| Is the text written in the past tense? | |
| What person is the text written in? First or third person? | |

# Report guide

## Animals in literature

A report gives the reader information about something.

Your report is going to be about the way animals are presented by the writers of the text extracts.

### Features of a report

- present tense
- third person
- non-chronological organisation
- factual writing

### Purpose

Why are you writing the report?

What do you want the reader to learn?

### Things to think about:

- the types of animals being written about;
- how we relate as humans to these animals;
- what the characteristics are that we like about these animals;
- how the writer presents the animals;
- whether or not the way the animals are described encourages us to see human characteristics in them;
- how we respond as readers to the animal.

*My report*

### Introduction

The introduction should tell the reader what you are going to write about.

### Development

After the introduction write about the following points:

- how the animals are presented to the reader;
- how the reader is persuaded that the animals are real.

### Conclusion

Finally, tell the reader how you think the writer has presented the animals to us.

Tell the reader what your response to the animals is.

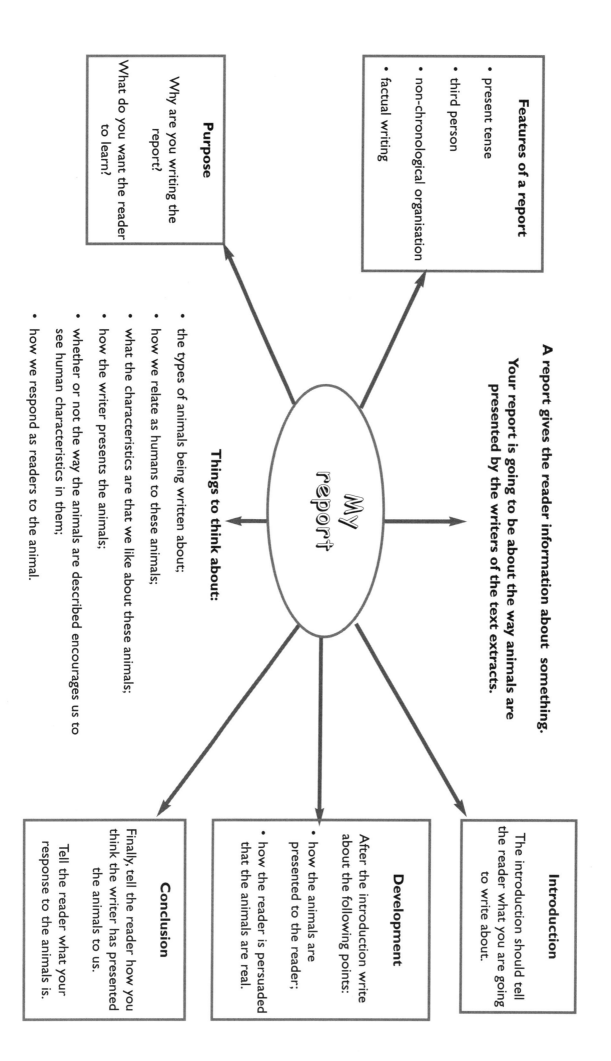

Animals in literature

## Language

Use persuasive language to convince the reader that your points of view are right.

Write in a formal style and use the third person.

Remember to use connectives such as 'however', 'on the other hand' and 'therefore' to develop your argument.

Make sure your spelling, punctuation and use of paragraphs are correct.

## Writer's purpose

Think about why you are writing:

• to inform?
• to persuade the reader to agree with you?

What ideas and information do you need to include?

## Remember:

You are putting forward your point of view.

**Question:**
Does the way animals are presented in stories influence the way we think about them?

## Reader's response

Do you think the reader will agree with your ideas?

## Content

What arguments are you going to present?

• **Introduction** – think about how to introduce the subject of how animals are portrayed in the texts.

• **Development** – think about how to organise the points you wish to make.

• **Conclusion** – think about how you will draw your ideas together to present your viewpoint and answer the question.

## Research

Think about what information the reader will need.

Think about what supporting evidence you will use to back up your viewpoint.

Remember to include scientific evidence from your research about real animals.

# Text extract

**from *Watership Down* by Richard Adams**

This extract describes Fiver and Hazel, their friends, and their encounter with bullies.

The first rabbit stopped in a sunny patch and scratched his ear with rapid movements of his hind-leg. Although he was a yearling and still below full weight, he had not the harassed look of most 'outskirters' – that is, the rank and file of ordinary rabbits in their first year who, lacking either aristocratic parentage or unusual size and strength, get sat on by their elders and live as best they can – often in the open – on the edge of their warren. He looked as though he knew how to take care of himself. There was a shrewd, buoyant air about him as he sat up, looked round and rubbed both front paws over his nose. As soon as he was satisfied that all was well, he laid back his ears and set to work on the grass.

His companion seemed less at ease. He was small, with wide, staring eyes and a way of raising and turning his head which suggested not so much caution as a kind of ceaseless, nervous tension. His nose moved continually and when a bumble-bee flew humming to a thistle bloom behind him, he jumped and spun round with a start that sent two nearby rabbits scurrying for holes before the nearest, a buck with black-tipped ears, recognised him and returned to feeding.

'Oh, it's only Fiver,' said the black-tipped rabbit, 'jumping at blue-bottles again. Come on, Buckthorn, what were you telling me?'

'Fiver?' said the other rabbit. 'Why's he called that?'

'Five in the litter, you know: he was the last – and the smallest. You'd wonder nothing had got him by now. I always say a man couldn't see him and a fox wouldn't want him. Still, I admit he seems to be able to keep out of harm's way.'

The small rabbit came closer to his companion, lolloping on long hind legs.

'Let's go a bit further, Hazel,' he said. 'You know, there's something queer about the warren this evening, although I can't tell exactly what it is. Shall we go down to the brook?'

'All right,' answered Hazel, 'and you can find me a cowslip. If you can't find one, no one can.'

He led the way down the slope, his shadow stretching behind him on the grass. They reached the brook and began nibbling and searching close beside the wheel-ruts of the track.

# Text extract

### from *Watership Down* by Richard Adams (cont)

It was not long before Fiver found what they were looking for. Cowslips are a delicacy among rabbits, and as a rule there are very few left by late May in the neighbourhood of even a small warren. This one had not bloomed and its flat spread of leaves was almost hidden under the long grass. They were just starting on it when two larger rabbits came running across from the other side of the near-by cattle wade.

'Cowslip?' said one. 'All right – just leave it to us. Come on, hurry up,' he added, as Fiver hesitated. 'You heard me, didn't you?'

'Fiver found it, Toadflax,' said Hazel.

'And we'll eat it,' replied Toadflax. 'Cowslips are for *Owsla* – don't you know that? If you don't, we can easily teach you.'

Fiver had already turned away. Hazel caught him up by the culvert.

'I'm sick and tired of it,' he said. 'It's the same all the time. "These are my claws, so this is my cowslip." "These are my teeth, so this is my burrow." I'll tell you, if ever i get into the Owsla, I'll treat outskirters with a bit of decency.'

'Well, you can at least expect to be in the Owsla one day,' answered Fiver. 'You've got some weight coming and that's more than I shall ever have.'

'You don't suppose I'll leave you to look after yourself, do you?' said Hazel. 'But to tell you the truth, I sometimes feel like clearing out of this warren altogether. Still, let's forget it now and try to enjoy the evening. I tell you what – shall we go across the brook? There'll be fewer rabbits and we can have a bit of peace. Unless you feel it isn't safe?' he added.

The way in which he asked suggested that he did in fact think that Fiver was likely to know better than himself, and it was clear from Fiver's reply that this was accepted between them.

'No, it's safe enough,' he answered. 'If I start feeling there's anything dangerous I'll tell you. But it's not exactly danger that I seem to feel about the place. It's – oh, I don't know – something oppressive, like thunder: I can't tell what; but it worries me. All the same, I'll come across with you.'

# Text extract

## from *Redwall* by Brian Jacques

This extract introduces Cluny the rat – leader of an army of destruction.

The high, warm sun shone on Cluny the Scourge.

Cluny was coming!

He was big, and tough; an evil rat with ragged fur and curved jagged teeth. He wore a black eyepatch; his eye had been torn out in battle with a pike.

Cluny had lost an eye.

The pike had lost its life!

Some said that Cluny was a Portuguese rat. Others said he came from the jungles far across the wide oceans. Nobody knew for sure.

Cluny was a bilge rat; the biggest, most savage rodent that ever jumped from ship to shore. He was black, with grey and pink scars all over his huge sleek body, from the tip of his wet nose, up past his green and yellow slitted eye, across both his mean tattered ears, down the length of his heavy vermin-ridden back to the enormous whip-like tail which had earned him his title: Cluny the Scourge!

Now he rode on the back of the hay wagon with his five hundred followers, a mighty army of rats: sewer rats, tavern rats, water rats, dockside rats. Cluny's army – fearing, yet following him. Redtooth, his second-in-command, carried a long pole. This was Cluny's personal standard, and the skull of a ferret was fixed at its top. Cluny had killed the ferret. He feared no living thing.

Wild eyed, with the terror of rat smell in its nostrils, the horse plunged ahead without any driver. Where the hay cart was taking him was of little concern to Cluny. Straight on the panicked horse galloped, past the mile-stone lodged in the earth at the roadside, heedless of the letters graven in the stone: 'Redwall Abbey, fifteen miles'.

Cluny was a God of War!

Cluny was coming nearer!...

...Cluny was in a foul temper. He snarled viciously.

The horse had stopped from sheer exhaustion. He hadn't wanted that: some inner devil persuaded him that he had not yet reached his destination. Cluny's one eye slitted evily.

# Text extract

**from *Redwall* by Brian Jacques (cont)**

From the depths of the hay cart the rodents of the Warlord's army watched their master. They knew him well enough to stay clear of him in his present mood. He was violent, unpredictable.

'Skullface,' Cluny snapped.

There was a rustle in the hay, a villainous head popped up.

'Aye, Chief, d'you want me?'

Cluny's powerful tail shot out and dragged the unfortunate forward. Skullface cringed as sharp dirty claws dug into his fur. Cluny nodded at the horse.

'Jump on that thing's back sharpish. Give it a good bite. That'll get the lazy brute moving again.'

Skullface swallowed nervously and licked his dry lips.

'But Chief, it might bite me back.'

Swish! Crack! Cluny wielded his mighty tail as if it were a bullwhip. His victim screamed aloud with pain as the scourge lashed his thin bony back.

'Mutiny, insubordination!' Cluny roared. 'By the teeth of hell, I'll flay you into mangy dollrags.'

Skullface scurried over on to the driver's seat, yelling with pain. 'No more! Don't whip me, Chief. Look, I'm going to do it.'

'Hold tight to the rigging back there,' Cluny shouted to his horde.

Skullface performed a frantic leap. He landed on the horse's back. The terrified animal did not wait for the rat to bite, as soon as it felt the loathsome scratching weight descend on its exposed haunches it gave a loud panicked whinny and bucked. Spurred on by the energy of fright it careered off like a runaway juggernaut.

Skullface had time for just one agonised scream before he fell. The iron-shod cartwheels rolled over him. He lay in a red mist of death, the life ebbing from his broken body. The last thing he saw before darkness claimed him was the sneering visage of Cluny the Scourge roaring from the jolting back-board, 'Tell the devil Cluny sent you, Skullface!'

They were on the move again. Cluny was getting nearer.

# Challenge 5

# Make a game

## Teacher's notes

### Purposes

- To help pupils develop their ability to deconstruct and analyse a text in detail.

- To use their analysis of a text to plan and develop ideas for a game related to the text. This will develop the ability to explain a procedure in terms of a series of sequences, instructions and rules.

- To develop reasoning skills.

- To develop thinking, planning and time management skills.

### Aims

- To read and deconstruct a text in detail.

- To use the information to develop a game that will help others understand the text.

### Resources required

The pupil will need copies of the following:

| | | |
|---|---|---|
| 1 | 'Challenge sheet' | page 112 |
| 2 | 'My action planning sheet' | page 113 |
| 3 | 'Task sheets' | pages 61 and 62 |
| 4 | 'Planning guidelines' | page 63 |
| 5 | 'Resources' sheet | page 64 |
| 6 | 'Text map' | page 65 |
| 7 | 'Important points' sheet | page 66 |
| 8 | 'Skills sheets' | page 114–117 |

### The teacher's role

#### 1  Introducing the challenge

Write the following in the top box of a copy of the 'Challenge sheet' (page 112):

*You are going to design a game based on a book you have read that will introduce other people to this book and help them understand it.*

*You need to select a suitable book, decide what type of game you are going to make and then plan and produce the game.*

Then photocopy the 'Challenge sheet' and give it to the pupils. Alternatively, they could be given a blank copy of the sheet and write the challenge on it themselves. It is important for them to have the challenge to refer to.

#### 2  Providing support for the task sheets

**Choosing the book**

Act as a guide in the selection of a book to use as a basis for developing the game in order to ensure it is suitable. For example, a game based on an Artemis Fowl story or a science fiction or fantasy novel would present the designer with opportunities to introduce the themes and characters of the text more easily than texts that tend to deal with more social issues. Pupils can be guided to the genre to use and texts can be set by the teacher if wished.

Questions that could be asked include:

- *'What kind (genre) of book do you think would be ideal for turning into a game – science fiction, adventure, fantasy, detective, mystery? Why?'*

- *'What is it about the book you have chosen that you think will make an interesting and challenging game?'*

- *'What age range is the book aimed at? Will this affect the type of game you design?'*

- *'Why do you think it would be beneficial for others to learn more about this book by playing the game?'*

**Using the 'Text map'**

This sheet is a way of showing pupils the main elements of their text quickly and effectively. The teacher could use this to begin a whole class activity that will allow the more able pupils to work independently while he or she works with the rest of the class. The sheet shows the pupils the areas of the text that they should identify. Able pupils should be encouraged to write in detail about the characters and their role in the text. The more able the pupil, the more detailed the mapping of the text should be.

The map encourages discussion based on the text and helps the pupils form an opinion about the writer's purpose. The map is a means of showing the pupils the elements that make up a text in terms of background – the place and the time. Teacher-led discussion will help the pupils realise the importance of context in a text. The reader is more able to make sense of the text if he or she understands the reason why the background and setting are appropriate for the narrative.

# Make a game

**Using the 'Important points' sheet**

If the whole class is doing this challenge, most could work together using the same text, while the more able select their own. The teacher could then use the 'Important points' sheet to demonstrate to the pupils how they can identify the factors that are important to the reader in helping them understand the development of the story. Any themes and issues raised and the development of the characters can be listed. The points listed can be used as a basis for developing the game about the text. The more able should be able to complete this sheet on their own with some guidance from the teacher.

**3 Other points to note**

Ensure the pupils understand that the game must introduce the players to the chosen text and must include themes from the text. There must be an objective (to finish first), difficulties to be overcome and rewards and penalties for players.

## Links to the National Curriculum

**English – Speaking and Listening**

*Level 5: Pupils talk effectively as members of a group, presenting and developing their ideas.*
*Level 6: Pupils take an active part in discussion, can summarise and develop points. Can consider alternative views and ideas and are sensitive to others.*

**English – Reading**

*Level 5: Pupils show understanding of the text. Can obtain specific information through thorough reading.*
*Level 6: Can comment on significant themes and issues in the text. Can give a personal response to the text. Can use a range of information from different sources.*

**English – Writing**

*Level 5: Can present written work in a format suitable for the purpose and the reader. Vocabulary choices suit the task. Spelling is generally accurate.*
*Level 6: Can discuss and evaluate written work. Can engage the reader's interest and use layout and language effectively.*

**Art and Design**

*Level 5: Ideas and visual information are explored to communicate ideas and meanings. Work is adapted to the purpose and meaning of the task set.*
*Level 6: Material is manipulated to communicate ideas. Work is analysed and developed to realise intentions.*

**Design and Technology**

*Level 5: Pupils work from plans and develop them for the purpose of the task set.*
*Level 6: Pupils check their design as it develops and evaluate and modify it in the light of their findings. They evaluate the product as it is used and identify ways of improving it.*

**PSHE and Citizenship KS2**

*2b – Pupils understand and discuss the need for rules in different situations and how they take part in making and changing rules.*

## Links to Literacy Framework
**Year 6, Term 3**

**Word level work**

*W3 – to use dictionaries and IT spellchecks to clarify meaning and spelling of new words.*

**Sentence level work**

*S1 – to revise language conventions and grammatical features of instructional texts.*

**Text level work**

*T22 – to select the appropriate style and form to suit a specific purpose and audience.*

# Assessment sheet

Make a game

Name: _____ Date: _____

| | Achieved | To achieve |
|---|---|---|
| **Speaking and Listening:** | | |

**Level 5:**
- Is effective in discussion as a member of a group.
- Can present and develop ideas.

**Level 6:**
- Takes an active part in discussion.
- Considers alternative views and ideas; is sensitive to others.

## Reading:

**Level 5:**
- Shows good understanding of the text chosen.
- Can obtain specific information through reading.

**Level 6:**
- Can comment on significant themes and issues in the text.
- Can use a range of information from different sources.

## Writing:

**Level 5:**
- Can present written work in a format suitable for the purpose.
- Vocabulary choices suit the tasks set.

**Level 6:**
- Can discuss and evaluate written work.
- Can use layout and language effectively.

## Art and Design:

**Level 5:**
- Ideas and visual information are used to communicate ideas and meanings.
- Work is adapted to the purpose and meaning of the task set.

**Level 6:**
- Material is manipulated to communicate ideas.
- Work is analysed and commented on.

## Design and Technology:

**Level 5:**
- Can work from plans and develop them for the purpose of the task set.

**Level 6:**
- Can evaluate design, modify it and improve it.

## PSHE and Citizenship:

- Understands the need for rules in different situations. Can take part in making and changing rules.

# Task sheet 1

## Exploring a text in detail

### Aim
To read a text and deconstruct it in detail.

### Tasks
- Use the **My action planning sheet** to help you plan your work.

- **Select a book** that you have read recently and that you think will be suitable to make into a game. Detective stories, fantasy novels or science fiction might be the best types of books for this task. **Discuss** the text with someone else. Explain to them why you think it will make a good game.

- Read and map out the text in detail using the **Text map**.

- Identify the themes that occur in the text. Think about why they are important to the story.

- Use the **Important points sheet** to make a list of all the important things you would tell someone about if you wanted him or her to read the story.

- **Make a list** of the key incidents in the story. Write an incident chart to remind you of the order they occur in (see below).

| incident | page | why the incident is important |
|----------|------|-------------------------------|
|          |      |                               |

- **Write a short summary** of the story: the themes and the characters in it.

- Use this work to help you with Task sheet 2.

# Task sheet 2

## Designing and making a game

### Aim

To design and make a game based on a book that will introduce other people to the text.

### Tasks

- Continue to use the **My action planning sheet** to help you plan your work.

- **Find out** about the different types of games people can play, such as board-games, quizzes and card games.

- **Use** the information you gathered doing Task sheet 1 to help you decide upon the type of game that you will design.

- **Plan** ideas for your game (refer to the **Planning guidelines**).

- **Draft** your game. Think carefully about the rules for the game. Make sure they can be easily followed.

- **Play** your game with a friend. Check that your rules and ideas work. Ask your friend if they learned anything about the book by playing the game.

- **Edit** your game and redevelop it until it works properly.

- **Make** a final version of the game.

## Extension work

- Design a box for your game which clearly indicates what type of game it is.

- Design an advertisement for your game. How would you make people want to buy it?

# Planning guidelines

## What to do

1. Read the task sheets carefully and then make your action plan of tasks to do and when to do them by completing the 'My action planning sheet'. Identify the skills you will demonstrate when carrying out the tasks. Are there any skills you need help with?

2. Carry out the speaking and listening tasks first so that you can analyse the text and decide whether or not the book will be suitable for making into a game.

3. Use the 'Text map' and the 'Important points' sheet to make a detailed summary of your chosen book.

4. Begin your research on different types of games. These could include:

   a) board-games;

   b) card games;

   c) quiz games.

5. Think carefully about the game you want to design.

   a) What will the objective of the game be? To achieve a goal? To save a life? To win something?

   b) What themes will you use in the game?

   c) Which characters from the book will you introduce?

   d) Will the players have to overcome difficulties based on incidents in the book?

   e) Will the game have tasks that involve the text? (You might give people a page reference and a task to perform, for example.)

6. Think very carefully about the rules for your game.

   a) How will players start?

   b) What do players have to do to finish/win?

   c) What rewards/penalties are given along the way? Is there a scoring system?

7. Make a draft of your game and play it with a friend. Are the rules clear and easy to understand? Do you need to change/improve anything? Did your friend learn anything about the book by playing the game?

8. Lastly, design and make a final version of your game. Think carefully about how you will present it so that it looks interesting and exciting to play.

| Internet | www.planet-kids.net/board-games.htm gives examples of different types of board games | Check 'Encarta' and similar other CD-Roms. |
|---|---|---|
| | Museum of Childhood at Bethnal Green www.vam.ac.uk/vastatic/nmc/ | |
| | Museum of Childhood Memories www.aboutbritain.com/museumofchildhood memories.htm | |
| | National Trust Museum of Childhood www.aboutbritain.com/nationaltrustmuseumof childhood.htm | |
| Speakers and other sources | Companies like John Waddington Ltd may send you information about designing games if you write to them. | Good local toy shops may help your research. |
| Libraries | Reference books and non-fiction books about designing games will be useful. | Ask the librarian to help you. |
| Visits | Local museums often have examples of how children played and may be able to help. | Trips can be an out of school activity as well as those organised by the school |
| | Museum of Childhood, Cambridge Heath Road, Bethnal Green, London E2 9PA, Tel 020 8980 2415, Fax 0208 983 5225 | |
| | Museum of Childhood, 42 High Street, Edinburgh EH1 1TG, Tel 0131 529 4142/4119, Fax 0131 558 3103 | |
| | Museum of Childhood Memories, 1 Castle Street, Beaumaris, Anglesey LL58 8AP, Tel 01248 712498 | |
| | National Trust Museum of Childhood, Sudbury Hall, Sudbury, Derbyshire DE6 5HT, Tel 01283 585 305 | |
| Your own ideas | Think about the games you enjoy. Are they fantasy role-play games, board-games, quiz type games? What type of game will suit the book you have selected? | Discuss your ideas with someone else. |

# Text map

Make a game

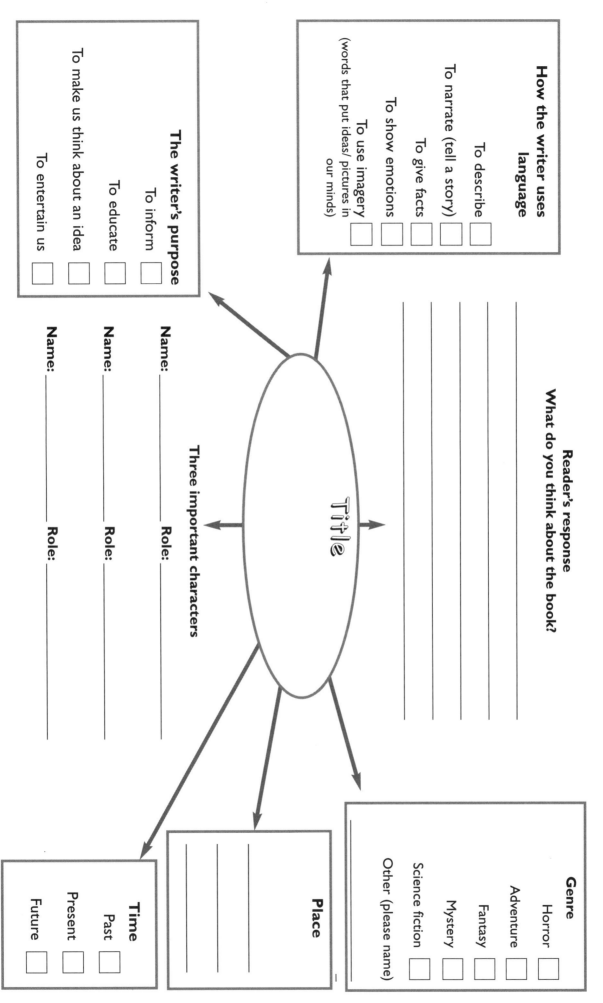

**How the writer uses language**

- To describe ☐
- To narrate (tell a story) ☐
- To give facts ☐
- To show emotions ☐
- To use imagery (words that put ideas/pictures in our minds) ☐

**The writer's purpose**

- To inform ☐
- To educate ☐
- To make us think about an idea ☐
- To entertain us ☐

**Reader's response**
**What do you think about the book?**

_____
_____
_____
_____
_____
_____

Title

**Three important characters**

Name: _____ Role: _____
Name: _____ Role: _____
Name: _____ Role: _____

**Place**

_____
_____
_____
_____

**Time**

- Past ☐
- Present ☐
- Future ☐

**Genre**

- Horror ☐
- Adventure ☐
- Fantasy ☐
- Mystery ☐
- Science fiction ☐
- Other (please name) ☐
  _____

# Important points

Make a game

List the important points the writer makes in the texts

| page reference | point made by the writer |
| --- | --- |
| | |

# Communications

## Teacher's notes

### Purposes

- To investigate how developments in communications technology have had an impact on our society in modern times.

- To develop reasoning skills.

- To develop thinking, planning and time management skills.

### Aims

- To investigate the impact on our lives of one form of communications technology.

- To write a newspaper article explaining how our lives have changed as a result of the developments in communications technology.

### Resource required

The pupil will need copies of the following:

| | | |
|---|---|---|
| 1 | 'Challenge sheet' | page 112 |
| 2 | 'My action planning sheet' | page 113 |
| 3 | 'Task sheets' | pages 70 and 71 |
| 4 | 'Planning guidelines' | page 72 |
| 5 | 'Resources' sheet | page 73 |
| 6 | 'Report guide' | page 74 |
| 7 | 'Newspaper article map' | page 75 |
| 8 | 'Skills sheets' | pages 114–177 |

### The teacher's role

#### 1 Introducing the challenge

Write the following in the top box of a copy of the 'Challenge sheet' (page 112):

*You are going to find out about how developments in communications technology have had an impact on our daily lives.*

*You are then going to choose one form of communications and write a newspaper article about how it has changed our lives in today's modern world.*

Then photocopy the 'Challenge sheet' and give it to the pupils. Alternatively, they could be given a blank copy of the sheet and write the challenge on it themselves. It is important for them to have the challenge to refer to.

#### 2 Providing support for the task sheets

#### Selecting a form of communications

Help the pupils to consider the communications listed on 'Task sheet 1' in order to decide which ones they think are the most useful and effective.

Questions that could be asked include:

- *'Which forms of communications do you and your family use the most? Why? How helpful are they in your daily lives? Which one couldn't you live without? Why?'*

- *'Now consider those forms that you have not used very much. Can you suggest how useful they might be to other people?'*

- *'Which form might be the most useful to people with certain handicaps, such as people with visual hearing impairments?'*

- *'Which form do you consider has made the most advances in recent years? How do you know this?'*

#### Using the 'Report guide'

This sheet can be used to help the pupils write their report as suggested in 'Task sheet 1'. The sheet provides a framework to develop a formal piece of writing. Teaching to write for a specific purpose is an important part of the process of developing the able pupil's ability to express his or her thinking in a structured and planned manner. Using this guide will provide them with a framework that can be adapted to other reports if required. Discuss the guide with the pupils and share their responses to the questions it raises.

#### Using the 'Newspaper article map'

This sheet is a means of reminding the pupil how a newspaper article is constructed and the areas that need consideration before writing begins. The purpose of the map is to encourage the pupils to deconstruct the task before embarking upon it. Use the map to lead a discussion about the different aspects of newspaper writing (articles and reports) and to guide the pupils in their planning.

## 3  Other points to note

'Task sheet 1' could be a whole class activity but the more able are expected to develop their ideas based on a thorough attempt to research for relevant information. Tracing the history of a chosen form of communications allows them to develop an understanding of the ways in which it has been developed and used by society.

The tasks on 'Task sheet 2' require them to use information gathered during the completion of 'Task sheet 1'. The survey carried out for 'Task sheet 2' could be a whole class activity. A visit to a newspaper office or from a journalist would make the process of writing a newspaper article more realistic and meaningful. Discuss the differences between a newspaper report and an article.

## Links to the National Curriculum

### English – Speaking and Listening

*Level 5: Pupils pay close attention to what others say.
The pupil makes a contribution to the discussion, taking into account the views of others.
Level 6: The pupil uses a variety of expressions to engage the listener's interest.
They can present their information using Standard English.*

### English – Reading

*Level 5: The pupil can select essential points from the text.
Relevant information is selected to support a viewpoint.
Level 6: A range of information can be summarised from a variety of sources.*

### English – Writing

*Level 5: Writing conveys meaning clearly.
Level 6: Writing is adapted to different forms.*

### History

*Level 5: Pupils show an increasing depth of factual knowledge.
Pupils can describe people, events and changes.
Level 6: Pupils can explain reasons for changes within a particular historical period.
The pupil is beginning to explain reasons for changes within a period of time.
The pupil is beginning to analyse historical interpretations of events and changes.*

### Science

*Level 5: Information is selected from a range of varied sources.
Level 6: Information from different sources is used effectively to explain and interpret evidence found in their recent research.*

## Links to Literacy Framework

### Year 6, Term 1

**Word level work**
*W3 – to use dictionaries and IT spellchecks.*

**Sentence level work**
*S5 – to form complex sentences.*

**Text level work**
*T11 – to distinguish between fact, opinion and fiction.
T13 – to secure understanding of the features of non-chronological reports.
T15 – to develop a journalistic style.
T16 – to use the styles and conventions of journalism.*

# Assessment sheet

Name: _____ Date: _____

| | Achieved | To achieve |
|---|---|---|
| **Speaking and Listening:**<br><br>**Level 5:**<br>• Can pay close attention to what others say.<br>• Makes a contribution, taking into account others' views.<br><br>**Level 6:**<br>• Uses a variety of expressions to engage the listener's interest.<br>• Presents information fluently using Standard English.<br><br>**Reading:**<br><br>**Level 5:**<br>• Can scan to select essential points from the text.<br>• Can select relevant information to support viewpoint.<br><br>**Level 6:**<br>• Can summarise a range of information from various sources.<br><br>**Writing:**<br><br>**Level 5:**<br>• Writing conveys meaning clearly.<br><br>**Level 6:**<br>• Writing is adapted to different forms.<br><br>**Science:**<br><br>**Level 5:**<br>• Information is selected from a range of varied sources.<br><br>**Level 6:**<br>• Information from different sources is used effectively to explain and interpret evidence found in their research.<br><br>**History:**<br><br>**Level 5:**<br>• Shows increasing depth of factual knowledge.<br>• Describes people, events and changes.<br><br>**Level 6:**<br>• Can explain reasons for changes within a period.<br>• Is beginning to analyse historical interpretations of events and changes. | | |

# Task sheet 1

## Investigating communications

### Aim

To investigate the impact on our lives of one form of communications technology.

### Tasks

- Use the **My action planning sheet** to help you plan your work.

- **Make a list** of all the ways that people can communicate with each other in today's world.

- Write down the types of technology that can be used to help people carry out the communications you have listed.

- **Choose** one form of communications technology and **find out** about how it was invented and improved over time. Then **write a report** on its invention and how it has developed to the present day. Use the **Report guide** to help you.

### Tip:

Here is a list of some of the forms of communications technology:
- telegraph
- land-line telephone
- mobile telephone
- radio
- television
- cinema/film
- internet
- email
- postal mail, letters
- satellite
- CD-Rom
- DVD
- video
- posters/advertisements
- publications – books, magazines, newspapers, leaflets
- creative media – painting, drawing, sculpture, collage

# Task sheet 2

## Writing a newspaper article

### Aim

To write a newspaper article explaining how our lives have changed as a result of one form of communications technology (you choose which one).

### Tasks

- Continue to use the **My action planning sheet** to help you plan your work.

- **Carry out** a survey to find the most popular forms of communications used by your family and friends.

- **Discuss** the information that has been presented in your group. What are your conclusions about the findings? What is the most popular method of communication chosen by your family and friends?

- **Use** the information you gathered about your chosen form of communications in Task 1 to help you **write a newspaper article** about how this form of communications has changed our lives.

- Use the **Newspaper article map** to help you plan and write your article. Make sure you select facts and opinions to help you present your article successfully.

- **Draft** an outline of your article showing the design and layout.

- Use a word processing program to produce your newspaper page.

## Extension work

- Carry out a survey of your class to find out which communications technology is the most popular. Explain why it is popular.
- Write a short story, entitled: 'Mountain Rescue' that highlights the importance of the mobile phone.

# Planning guidelines

## What to do

1. Read the task sheets carefully and then make up your action plan of tasks to do and when to do them by completing the 'My action planning sheet'. Identify the skills you will demonstrate when carrying out the tasks. Are there any skills you need help with?

2. Carry out the research tasks first so that you have the information you need for your group discussion and presentation.

3. Remember to keep a record of your sources of information in case you need to refer to them again.

4. When writing your report, use the 'Report guide' to help you.

5. Make sure you plan in detail before you start your newspaper article. You should make sure you have all the information you need before you start writing.

6. Remember you are presenting your point of view. Think about your choice of communications technology and the impact it has had on people's lives before you begin to plan and write.

7. Have you found all the scientific information you need to help you write a well-informed newspaper article?

8. Check your draft article and edit it carefully before you produce your final piece. If you are word processing your work, include pictures downloaded from the computer.

9. Try to ensure that your newspaper article presents your answer to the question in a way that will persuade the reader to agree with you.

Read all about it!

# Resources

| | | |
|---|---|---|
| **Internet** | A timeline of 20th century inventions<br>*http://inventors.about.com/library/weekly/aa121599a.htm*<br><br>Inventors and inventions:<br><br>Radio<br>*http://www.inventors.about.com/library/inventors/blradio.htm*<br><br>Telephone<br>*http://www.inventors.about.com/library/inventors/bltelephone.htm* | 'Encarta' and other like sources may help. |
| **Speakers and other sources** | Find out if there is a local museum with communications technology displays – they could provide a speaker for the class.<br>The communications officer in the army.<br>Local radio or television journalists. | Good local technology shops may help your research. |
| **Libraries** | The reference section will have books on the various inventions you wish to research. | Librarians will help you find what you need. |
| **Visits** | A local airport, police station or fire station will be able to show you how they use communications technology.<br>Newspaper offices and journalists. | A school visit or private visit can be organised. |
| **Audience** | Talk to people who use communications technology; include family and friends. Do they think your choice has changed the way we live? | Make up a survey; ask at least ten people. |
| **Your own ideas** | Think about the impact of the technology and how a journalist would write about it. | Discuss your ideas with your teacher and friends. |

# Report guide

## Communications

**Features of a report**

present tense

third person

non-chronological organisation

factual writing

**Purpose**

The purpose of the report is to:

- identify the communications technology being used;

- make sure the reader understands its impact in the world today.

A report gives the reader information about something.

**Your report is going to be about one form of communications technology.**

**Describe how it was invented and how it has developed until its use today.**

My report

**Things to think about:**

Which communications technology are you most interested in?

Where can you find information about it that will give you an outline of its history? (Use the Resources sheet to help you.)

What are the key points in its development?

What points and illustrations will you need to include in your report?

## Introduction

The introduction should tell the reader what you are going to write about.

Say why you have chosen this particular form of communications.

## Development

After the introduction write about the following points:

- Who invented it? When?
- What major developments occurred to this form of communications over the years?

## Conclusion

Finally, tell the reader how the technology is used today.

Tell the reader what your response to the technology is and what you think the future for it will be.

Communications

## Purpose

To tell readers how our lives have been changed as a result of one form of communications.

### Language

Use persuasive language to convince the reader that your points of view are right.

Write in a formal style and use the third person.

Include facts in your article.

Write in a style that makes it obviously a newspaper article.

### Writer's purpose

Think about what you wish your reader to conclude after reading your article.

What knowledge do you wish them to acquire?

### Remember:

You decide which form of communications technology to write about.

You are putting forward your point of view.

### Content

What arguments are you going to present?

- **Introduction** – think about how to introduce your opinion about this form of communication.
- **Development** – think about how to organise the points you wish to make. List the points you will use and number them to make sure you use them in the right order
- **Conclusion** – think about how you will draw your ideas together to present your viewpoint.

### Layout

Think about:
- title;
- pictures;
- captions;
- fonts.

### Reader's response

Do you think the reader will agree with your ideas?

### Research

Think about what information the reader will need.

Think about what supporting evidence you will use to back up your viewpoint.

# Challenge 7

# Ethics

## Teacher's notes

### Purposes

- To investigate the idea of ethics and how it affects us.
- To explore fundamental questions in a creative way.
- To investigate the meaning of words.
- To develop thinking, planning and time management skills.

### Aims

- To discuss the meaning of the term 'justice' and write a discussion text about it.
- To write a playscript that explains to others what an ethical approach to the care of the elderly can be.

### Resources required

The pupil will need copies of the following:

| | | |
|---|---|---|
| 1 | 'Challenge sheet' | page 112 |
| 2 | 'My action planning sheet' | page 113 |
| 3 | 'Task sheets' | pages 79 and 80 |
| 4 | 'Planning guidelines' | page 81 |
| 5 | 'Resources' sheet | page 82 |
| 6 | 'Discussion text guide' | page 83 |
| 7 | 'Playscript guide' | page 84 |
| 8 | 'Skills sheets' | pages 114–117 |

### The teacher's role

#### 1 Introducing the challenge

Write the following in the top box of a copy of the 'Challenge sheet' (page 112):

*You are going to find out what the meaning of the term 'justice' is.*

*You are then going to write a playscript that explains to the audience what an ethical approach to the care of the elderly could be.*

Then photocopy the 'Challenge sheet' and give it to the pupils. Alternatively, they could be given a blank copy of the sheet and write the challenge on it themselves. It is important for them to have the challenge to refer to.

#### 2 Providing support for the task sheets

**Finding out what the term 'justice' means**

Discussion plays a very important part in this challenge and the teacher will need to ensure that boundaries for discussions are agreed and adhered to before the discussions begin. The following points could be taken into consideration:

- Listen attentively and respectfully to what others have to say.
- Try to ask questions that will develop the discussion.
- Remember that others may have different points of view to you and that their ideas are equally as valid as yours.
- Do not interrupt when others are speaking.
- Do not mock or put down another person's ideas.
- Put forward your own ideas in a polite and calm manner to ensure that others will listen to your point of view.
- Keep an open mind – someone else may be able to change the way you think about things!

The questions on 'Task sheet 1' need to be considered and discussed in depth. The pupils should address their comments to each other, not the teacher. The teacher, however, should keep an eye on the progress of the discussions and, perhaps, intervene when the talk seems to be lagging. Questions to promote more in-depth discussion could include:

- *'How do you think you have learned about words such as 'freedom', 'truth' and 'justice'? Who or what has influenced your ideas?'*
- *'Why do you think people have different ideas about what these words mean? How do you think their ideas have been developed/shaped?'*
- *'Do you think you might have different ideas about these terms if you lived in a different country? Why/ why not?'*
- *'Why do you think the National Curriculum document for schools has such a statement in it?'*

The first part of 'Task sheet 1' could be carried out as a whole class discussion. The more able could then continue to work in more depth while the others in the class could work with the teacher to agree a definition of 'justice' together.

The teacher could then introduce and develop the concept of ethics to the pupils if he or she wishes to; for example, work ethics, game playing ethics and so on.

## Using the 'Discussion text guide'

This sheet enables the pupils to plan their writing in a structured way. The emphasis is on the need to decide what ideas and information should be included in order to present their point of view in the most effective way.

Read the sheet through with the pupils before they commence in order to ensure they understand the task.

## Using the 'Playscript guide'

This sheet will be a useful guide to the pupils when planning their playscript. The teacher may need to support pupils in deciding the issues they wish to raise in the course of the play and how they can best present these to an audience. This will be a very challenging task but it is one that the more able pupils should readily rise to because it will test their creative skills to the limit.

## 3 Other points to note

Firm deadlines will need to be provided by the teacher to help the pupils develop their priorities when researching for information and planning their writing.

The teacher's role for 'Task sheet 2' is to help the pupils investigate the term 'ethics' and decide on its meaning. The main part of the task is to use this definition of ethics and apply it to the care of the elderly in our society. The pupils will need support in investigating what the current care provisions are for the elderly. They will also need help in trying to understand what the problems of the elderly might be. Many young people highly value their relationships with their own grandparents and elderly friends so this should be a good starting point from which to begin their investigations.

Pupils may draw different conclusions from their teachers and each other about the ethics of elderly care. The important point is that the pupils should be encouraged to present all their ideas in a reasonable and respectful manner. Pupils can agree to disagree!

## Links to the National Curriculum

### English – Speaking and Listening

*Level 5: Pupils talk confidently in a range of contexts.*
*They listen closely to what others say.*
*They develop answers and make contributions that take into account others' views.*
*Level 6: Pupils adapt talk to the demands of the different contexts.*
*They take an active part in discussions.*
*They show an understanding of the ideas of others.*

### English – Reading

*Level 5: Pupils select essential points from a range of texts.*
*They select relevant information to support their views.*
*Level 6: Pupils can identify different layers of meaning and comment on their significance.*
*They can summarise a range of information from different sources.*

### English – Writing

*Level 5: Pupils' writing is varied and interesting.*
*Level 6: Pupils' writing adapts to different forms of style and register.*

### PSHE and Citizenship – KS2

*Pupils show an understanding of moral and social problems.*
*They share their opinions on things that matter to them and explain their views.*
*They can meet and talk with people.*

### National Curriculum Statement of Values

*Pupils show others that they are valued and show the need to understand and support others.*

## Links to Literacy Framework

### Year 6, Term 1

**Word level work**
*W3 – to use dictionaries and IT spellchecks.*

**Sentence level work**
*S1 – to adapt texts for different purposes.*

**Text level work**
*T9 – to prepare a playscript using stage directions and location/setting.*

# Assessment sheet

Ethics

Name: _____ Date: _____

| | Achieved | To achieve |
|---|---|---|
| **Speaking and Listening:** | | |

## Speaking and Listening:

**Level 5:**

- Talks confidently in a range of contexts.
- Can listen with close attention to what others say.
- Develops answers and makes contributions that take into account others' views.

**Level 6:**

- Adapts his or her talk to the demands of the different contexts.
- Takes an active part in discussion.
- Is sensitive to the ideas of others.
- Shows an understanding of the ideas of others.

## Reading:

**Level 5:**

- Selects essential points from a range of texts.
- Selects relevant information to support his/her views.

**Level 6:**

- Can identify different layers of meaning and comment on their significance.
- Can summarise a range of information from different sources.

## Writing:

**Level 5:**

- Writing is varied and interesting.

**Level 6:**

- Writing adapts to different forms of style and register.

## PSHE:

- Shows an understanding of moral and social problems.
- Can share opinions on things that matter to them and explain their views.
- Can meet and talk with people.

## Statement of Values:

- Shows others that they are valued and understands the need to support others.

# Task sheet 1

## Finding out about the term 'justice'

### Aim

To discuss the meaning of the term 'justice' and write a discussion text about it.

### Tasks

- Use the **My action planning sheet** to help you plan your work.

- **Read** the following sentence, which comes from the Statement of Values in the National Curriculum handbook for teachers:

  'We value <u>truth</u>, <u>freedom</u>, justice, <u>human rights</u>, the <u>rule of law</u> and <u>collective effort</u> for the <u>common good</u>.'
  (The National Curriculum Handbook for Key Stages 1 and 2, page 148)

- In a group, **choose** one of the words or phrases underlined in this statement. Look it up in a dictionary and write down the meaning given. Does your group agree with this meaning? Write down what your group decides.

- In pairs, **discuss** the word 'justice'. What do you think it means? DO NOT use a dictionary this time to look up its meaning.

  In your discussion, consider the following:

  - Can you give an example of what justice is?
  - Do we need justice in our society?
  - Can you give reasons for your answer?
  - Do you and the others in the group have the same ideas about the meaning of 'justice'?
  - Is it important to respect the ideas of others? Why?

- Still in your pairs, **prepare a short role play** to show others in your group what you think 'justice' means.

- Use the things you have found out in your discussions and through watching the role plays to **write** a discussion text about what you think justice is. You may have to do some more research. Use the **Discussion text guide** to help you.

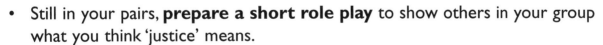

# Task sheet 2

## Writing a playscript

### Aim

To write a playscript that explains to the audience what an ethical approach to the care of the elderly could be.

### Tasks

* Continue to use the **My action planning sheet** to help you plan your work.

* With a partner, **discuss** what you think the term 'ethics' means and write it down. Use dictionaries and information books to help you. **Share** your ideas with others in your group and with your teacher.

* **Find out** how the elderly can be cared for today in our society. Find out what problems the elderly can face today and how they can be helped. Use the **Resources sheet** to help you. Write your findings in note form.

* Use your notes to help you **plan** out a play that will tells others about an ethical approach to the care of the elderly. Use the **Playscript guide** to help you.

* **Act out** your play to others.

## Extension work

* Design an area in a park that could be used for the elderly. What kinds of facilities do you think they would need? Think about rest and recreation.

# Planning guidelines

## What to do

1. Read the task sheets carefully and then make up your action plan of tasks to do and when to do them by completing the 'My action planning sheet'. Identify the skills you will demonstrate when carrying out the tasks. Are there any skills you need help with?

2. When you are discussing things with a partner or in a group remember the following points:

   a) It is important to let everyone have a turn.

   b) Listen to each other respectfully.

   c) Other people may have different views to you so think carefully about what they have to say – they might change the way you think about things.

   d) Put forward your ideas in a polite and calm way.

3. When writing up your ideas about 'justice' use the 'Discussion guide' to help you. Think back to your discussions – what did you learn from listening to the views of others in the group? Have your ideas about the meaning of justice changed as a result?

4. To define the word 'ethics' you need to use more than one source to decide on its meaning. Start with a dictionary and then move on to an encyclopaedia. You could also carry out a survey to see what others think.

5. Use the 'Resources' sheet to help you find information about the problems of the elderly and how they are cared for in today's society.

6. When writing your script think about:

   a) listing the points you need to make;

   b) how you will plan and organise your ideas;

   c) the drafting, editing and practising of the script;

   d) how you will present the play.

   Use the 'Playscript guide' to help you.

# Resources

| Internet | Use information CDs to research words like 'ethics' and key words in the task sheets.<br><br>http://schools.helptheaged.org.uk/_schools/default.htm | Try CD-Rom encyclopaedias |
|---|---|---|
| **Speakers and other sources** | Various people who work with others, such as social workers, the police or the nurse for elderly care in the community, may visit and discuss your questions with you.<br><br>Try Age Concern and Help the Aged. | Contact by writing or phoning. |
| **Libraries** | Texts, both fiction and non-fiction, may help you to develop your thoughts and ideas. | The librarian will help you. |
| **Visits** | Small groups could visit a retirement home for the elderly to find out how care is given and if there are rules and regulations to follow.<br>Visit elderly friends and talk to them. | Write to ask if you can visit. |
| **Audience** | Your peers are your audience; ask them your questions and find out what they think. How can you get your ideas across to them in your play? | Parents and relatives may be able to help with ideas and opinions. |
| **Your own ideas** | You have questions to think about and try to answer. Your ideas and views may be different from your friends'. Your experience of life will help you to develop your ideas. | Discuss your ideas with friends and your teacher. |

# Discussion text guide

Ethics

## Language

Use persuasive language to encourage the reader to respond positively to your ideas.

Write in a formal style and use the third person.

Remember to use connectives such as 'however', 'on the other hand' and 'therefore' to develop your point of view.

Use facts to give accurate explanations.

## Themes and issues

Do you have a message about justice for the reader?

Are you trying to make them think about the meaning of the word?

Are you trying to show them what justice is?

**Remember:**

You are putting forward your point of view.

## Question: What is justice?

## Reader's response

What do you want the reader to think about justice?

## Content

**Introduction** – this paragraph should define the word and introduce your idea of what justice is.

**Development** – explain which ideas were discussed and what sense you made of them through your research.

**Conclusion** – comment on your ideas about justice. Have they changed?

## Research

Think about what information the reader will need.

Use dictionaries, encyclopaedias and notes from discussions.

Talk to people who are involved with the justice system you have in school – how do they define justice?

A playscript tells the actors what to say and how to say it.

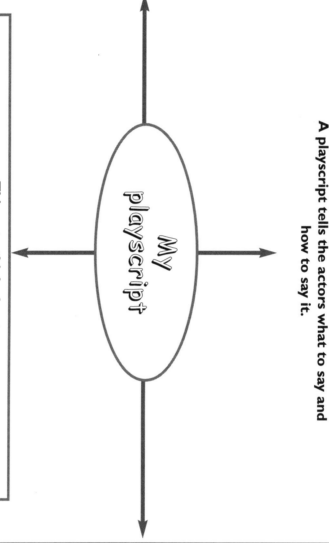

**My playscript**

## Language

Think about the types of language you will use:

- descriptive – to set the scene;
- dialogue – to show the conversations between the characters, their thoughts and ideas.
- factual – to introduce the ideas and information you want the audience to think about.

## Features of a playscript

The work is divided into large sections called 'Acts' and then into smaller sections called 'Scenes'.

The scene setting is written in italics. It tells us where the characters are and what props they will need.

The characters' names are written in capitals down the left-hand side of the page. Next to each name is the dialogue they speak.

Sometimes words are written in brackets to indicate how the dialogue is spoken.

Stage directions are written in italics in brackets.

## Things to think about:

- What is an ethical approach?
- What are the needs and problems of the elderly?
- Is there a need for an ethical approach to the care of the elderly?
- How can a play explain the needs and problems of the elderly?
- What information do you want to tell the audience?
- How many characters will the play have?
- How will you make the play interesting?
- What do you want your audience to learn from watching the play?

# Keeping fit

## Teacher's notes

### Purposes

- To investigate how health is maintained through nutrition and exercise.

- To develop investigation and analytical skills.

- To plan how to present facts and ideas using appropriate language.

- To develop thinking, planning and time management skills.

### Aims

- To find out how the human body can be kept healthy.

- To produce a leaflet that outlines a health and fitness programme for a young person.

### Resources required

The pupil will need copies of the following:

| | | |
|---|---|---|
| 1 | 'Challenge sheet' | page 112 |
| 2 | 'My action planning sheet' | page 113 |
| 3 | 'Task sheets' | pages 88 and 89 |
| 4 | 'Planning guidelines' | page 90 |
| 5 | 'Resources' sheet | page 91 |
| 6 | 'Report guide' | page 92 |
| 7 | 'Leaflet guide' | page 93 |
| 8 | 'Skills sheets' | pages 114–117 |

### The teacher's role

#### 1 Introducing the challenge

Write the following into the top box of a copy of the 'Challenge sheet' (page 112):

*You are going to find out how the human body can be kept healthy.*

*You are then going to design and make a leaflet that outlines a health and fitness programme for a fortnight for a person who is a year younger than you.*

Then photocopy the 'Challenge sheet' and give it to the pupils. Alternatively, they could be given a blank copy of the sheet and write the challenge on it themselves. It is important for them to have the challenge to refer to.

#### 2 Providing support for the task sheets

**Finding out how to keep the human body healthy**
This part of the challenge (see 'Task sheet 1') could be teacher-led as a whole class activity that incorporates aspects of PSHE, Science and PE.

Find out what the pupils already know about nutrition and exercise in order to direct them towards the appropriate areas of research that they still need to carry out. Putting the pupils into groups to discuss what people should do to keep fit and then asking them to report back to the teacher will help identify their previous knowledge and its accuracy.

**Using the 'Report guide'**
This sheet can be used to help the pupils write their report as suggested on 'Task sheet 1'. It provides a framework to develop a formal piece of writing. Teaching to write for a specific purpose is an important part of the process of developing the able pupil's ability to express his or her thinking in a structured and planned manner. Using this 'Report guide' will provide pupils with a framework that can be adapted to other reports if required.

Discuss the guide with the pupils and encourage them to make notes for each part of their report.

**Using the 'Leaflet guide'**
This sheet will be a useful guide to the pupils when planning their leaflet. It outlines all the things that need to be taken into consideration and reminds the pupils of the purpose of the writing.

Provide the pupils with a selection of leaflets for them to discuss and evaluate so that they can list the features of a 'good' leaflet and incorporate these features into their own design. Discuss the type of language used in leaflets and how a good layout can influence the reader positively.

#### 3 Other points to note

Firm deadlines will need to be provided to help the pupils develop their priorities when researching for information and planning their writing.

The teacher's role for 'Task sheet 2' is to help the pupils sort the information they have gathered from 'Task sheet 1' into a healthy eating and exercise programme that can be followed logically by a younger person. How effective do they think the programme will be if followed over a period of time? (A whole class challenge might be to choose one of the programmes and follow it over several months to monitor it!)

The teacher will need to discuss with the pupils their ideas about how the leaflet should look and what should be included in it. Will diagrams be used? What ICT program will be used to lay out the leaflet? How much help will individuals need in using the program?

Guidance should be provided with the costings element of the programme. What things in the programme will need to be costed out? What do they need to do in order to find out costs? How useful will spreadsheets be?

## Links to the National Curriculum

### English – Speaking and Listening

*Level 5: Pupils can make contributions to discussion and develop ideas taking into account the views of others.*
*Level 6: Pupils can take an active part in discussions and show understanding of the ideas and views of others.*

### English – Reading

*Level 5: Pupils can identify fact and opinion, selecting essential points from a range of sources.*
*Level 6: Pupils can summarise a range of information from different sources.*

### English – Writing

*Level 5: Pupils can convey meaning clearly in a range of forms.*
*Level 6: Pupils' writing engages and sustains the reader's interest, showing some adaptation of style and register to different forms.*

### Maths – Using and Applying Mathematics

*Level 5: Pupils can identify and obtain necessary information.*
*Level 6: Pupils carry through tasks and solve problems by independently breaking them down into manageable tasks.*

### Maths – Number and Algebra

*Level 5: Pupils can solve problems using number skills.*
*Level 6: Pupils show the ability to solve 'real life' problems using a variety of number calculations.*

### Science

*Level 5: Pupils demonstrate knowledge of life processes.*
*Level 6: Pupils use their scientific knowledge to explain life processes.*

### ICT

*Level 5: Information can be selected for different purposes.*
*Level 6: Pupils can present information in a variety of ways and show a clear sense of audience.*

### PE

*Level 5: Pupils can explain why regular exercise is good for their fitness and health.*
*Level 6: Pupils can explain how different types of exercise contribute to their fitness and health. They describe how they can get involved in activities and exercise.*

### PSHE and Citizenship – KS2

*Developing a healthy, safer lifestyle:*
*Pupils show an understanding of what makes a healthy lifestyle. They can demonstrate the benefits of healthy eating.*

## Links to Literacy Framework

### Year 6, Term 3

### Word level work

*W3 – to use dictionaries and IT spellchecks.*

### Sentence level work

*S2 – to understand the features of official language.*

### Text level work

*T17 – to understand examples of official language and its characteristic features.*
*T20 – to discuss the way Standard English varies in different contexts.*

# Assessment sheet

Keeping fit

Name: _____ Date: _____

|  | Achieved | To achieve |
|---|---|---|
| **Speaking and Listening:**<br><br>**Level 5:**<br>• Makes contributions and develops ideas.<br>**Level 6:**<br>• Takes an active part in discussion; understands the ideas of others.<br><br>**Reading:**<br><br>**Level 5:**<br>• Can identify key features of fact and opinion.<br>**Level 6:**<br>• Summarises information from a range of sources.<br><br>**Writing:**<br><br>**Level 5:**<br>• Can convey meaning clearly in a range of forms.<br>**Level 6:**<br>• Adapts style and register to different forms.<br><br>**Science:**<br><br>**Level 5:**<br>• Demonstrates knowledge of life processes.<br>**Level 6:**<br>• Uses knowledge to explain life processes.<br><br>**PSHE:**<br><br>• Shows understanding of what makes a healthy lifestyle.<br>• Demonstrates the benefits of healthy eating.<br><br>**PE:**<br><br>**Level 5:**<br>• Can explain why regular exercise is good for fitness and health.<br>**Level 6:**<br>• Can explain how different types of exercise can contribute to fitness and health. |  |  |

# Task sheet 1

## Finding out what keeps us healthy

**Aim**

To find out how the human body can be kept healthy.

**Tasks**

- Use the **My action planning sheet** to help you plan your work.

- **Discuss** with someone in your group what you think people should do in order to stay fit and healthy. Do you know what foods we should eat? Do you know what types of exercise can build strength and stamina? Make a note of your ideas.

- **Find out** how nutrition helps the human body to remain healthy. Find out about:

  - the types of food we need to eat;
  - how food is divided into different categories and how much of each we need to eat to maintain a healthy diet;
  - which types of food help our brain, our muscles and our skeleton.

  Collect as much information as you can and keep it in a folder.

- **Find out** about the types of exercise we can do to stay healthy. Find out:

  - whether children should do the same exercise as adults;
  - how often we should exercise and for how long;
  - the different types of exercise and how they can help to build stamina and strength in different parts of our body.

  Make a note of your findings and add this to your folder.

- Use what you have found out to **write** a report on what humans need to stay fit and healthy. Use the **Report guide** to help you.

# Task sheet 2

## Writing a leaflet

### Aim

To plan, design and use ICT to produce a leaflet that outlines a health and fitness programme for a fortnight for a person one year younger than you.

### Tasks

• Continue to use the **My action planning sheet** to help you plan your work.

• **Use your report** from 'Task sheet 1' to help you plan the programme. You need to include:

– a **keep fit programme** of exercise suitable for the age group you are writing for that will help develop stamina and strength;

– a **menu of food and drink** for a fortnight that will help the young   person stay healthy;

– how much the programme will **cost** for the fortnight.

• **Plan** a leaflet that will tell the young person about the health and fitness programme. Use the **Leaflet guide** to help you. Think about:

– how you will set it out to make it interesting to read;

– how to make sure the text is at the right reading level for the age of the person it is aimed at;

– what information and diagrams you will use.

• **Use an ICT program** to produce your leaflet. **Edit** and **correct** your final draft.

• **Publish** and **present** your programme to others in your group.

## Extension work

• Carry out a survey of your class to find out what fitness activities they do. Make a bar chart of your results. Find out how much time they spend watching television. Does your class need to do more exercise?

# Planning guidelines

## What to do

1. Read the task sheets carefully and then make up your action plan of tasks to do and when to do them by completing the 'My action planning sheet'. Identify the skills you will demonstrate when carrying out the tasks. Are there any skills you need help with?

2. Use the 'Resources' sheet to help you find out about nutrition and types of exercise suitable for the age group you are aiming the leaflet at.

3. Make notes of the main points you feel people need to know about in order to stay healthy. Take copies of any diagrams you find that you think will be useful in your leaflet. Keep a record of the sources of your information in case you need to refer to them again later.

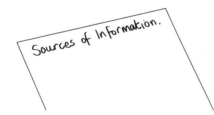

4. When you write your report remember to think carefully about its purpose and use the 'Report guide' to help you.

5. When planning the leaflet think carefully about what information you should include in it. (Use the 'Leaflet guide'.) The text needs to be long enough to include all the important details but not so long that the reader loses interest. You also need to consider the sort of advice you will give the reader to help them keep to the programme!

6. When designing the leaflet consider the following:

   a) which ICT program you will use;

   b) how you will lay out the information. What headings will you use? Will you use boxes?

   c) the fonts you will use to create the best effects;

   d) what type of visual information you will use – tables, charts, diagrams, drawings, cartoons;

   e) the order in which you will present the information.

Keeping fit

# Resources

| Internet | Nutrition:<br>www.galaxy-h.gov.uk/balance-of-good-health.html<br><br>British Heart Foundation:<br>www.bhf.org.uk<br><br>General information on healthy eating:<br>Food is fun: fitness and food<br>www.foodisfun.co.uk | Try CD-Rom encyclopaedias. |
|---|---|---|
| **Speakers and other sources** | Nurses, nutritionists and fitness trainers would be interesting speakers with good information. The British Heart Foundation might send information that would help. | Contact by writing or phoning. |
| **Libraries** | Reference books on biology, the human body, nutrition fitness should be helpful sources of information. | The librarian will help you. |
| **Visits** | Fitness centres and shops to check where healthy food is sold. | These can be individual or group visits. Discuss places to visit with friends. |
| **Audience** | Younger people who need information about a healthy lifestyle. Ask them for their ideas; they could be helpful. | |
| **Your own ideas** | List your ideas. Think about the cost of them. Could people afford your programme? | Discuss your ideas with friends and your teacher. |

# Report guide

Keeping fit

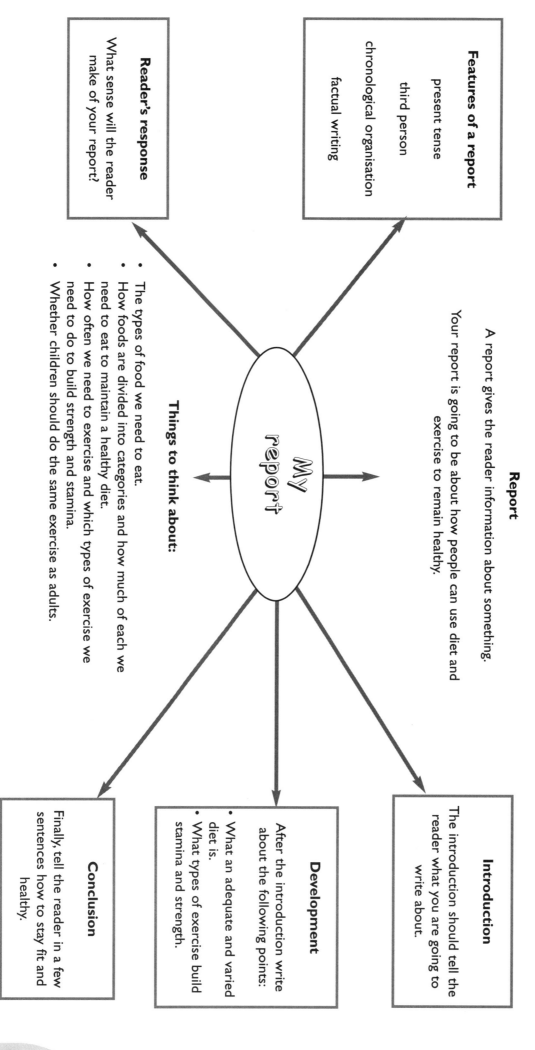

**Features of a report**

present tense

third person

chronological organisation

factual writing

**Reader's response**

What sense will the reader make of your report?

**Things to think about:**

- The types of food we need to eat.
- How foods are divided into categories and how much of each we need to eat to maintain a healthy diet.
- How often we need to exercise and which types of exercise we need to do to build strength and stamina.
- Whether children should do the same exercise as adults.

**Report**

A report gives the reader information about something.

Your report is going to be about how people can use diet and exercise to remain healthy.

*My report*

**Introduction**

The introduction should tell the reader what you are going to write about.

**Development**

After the introduction write about the following points:

- What an adequate and varied diet is.
- What types of exercise build stamina and strength.

**Conclusion**

Finally, tell the reader in a few sentences how to stay fit and healthy.

## Language

Use persuasive language to encourage the reader to agree with your ideas and follow the programme.

Use factual, official language to try and convince the reader of the importance of your programme.

## Writer's purpose

Think about what you wish your reader to conclude after reading your article.

What knowledge do you wish them to acquire?

## ICT

Decide which program you will use to produce a good leaflet.

## Purpose

To tell readers how to follow a health and fitness programme to stay healthy.

## Reader's response

Do you think the reader will be able to follow your programme successfully?

## Content

Think about:
- the facts about healthy eating;
- the facts about the types of suitable exercises for the age group you are targeting;
- the order of the points in the programme;
- where and when the eating and exercise should take place and how often;
- the amounts of food/exercise that are ideal;
- how much the programme will cost.

## Layout

Think about:
- fonts;
- headings;
- captions;
- use of diagrams/drawings;
- where the information will be placed.

Plan your layout on paper and then on the computer.

## Research

Think about what information the reader will need.

Think about what supporting evidence you will use to back up your programme.

# Challenge 9

# The local area

## Teacher's notes

### Purposes

- To find out about the history of the local area.

- To trace the local area's development over a specific time period.

- To develop thinking, planning and time management skills.

### Aims

- To find out about the history of the place where you live.

- To write a story about an invented character based on research into a specific time period in the local area.

### Resources required

The pupil will need copies of the following:

| | | |
|---|---|---|
| 1 | 'Challenge sheet' | page 112 |
| 2 | 'My action planning sheet' | page 113 |
| 3 | 'Task sheets' | pages 97 and 98 |
| 4 | 'Planning guidelines' | page 99 |
| 5 | 'Resources' sheet | page 100 |
| 6 | 'Summary guide' | page 101 |
| 7 | 'Character map' | page 102 |
| 8 | 'Story map' | page 103 |
| 9 | 'Skills sheets' | pages 114–117 |

### The teacher's role

#### 1  Introducing the challenge

Write the following in the top box of a copy of the 'Challenge sheet' (page 112):

*You are going to find out about the history of our (village, town, city, county) during the time of the (Victorians, Tudors, 1930s, Romans). (The teacher chooses the period.)*

*You are then going to invent a local character who lived here during this time and write a story about him or her.*

Then photocopy the 'Challenge sheet' and give it to the pupils. Alternatively, they could be given a blank copy of the sheet and write the challenge on it themselves. It is important for them to have the challenge to refer to.

#### 2  Providing support for the task sheets

**Finding out about the local area during the chosen time period**

This part of the challenge (see 'Task sheet 1') could be carried out as a whole class activity. More able pupils should be able to develop their own lines of research, working together or independently without too much help, whereas other pupils may need more support. The teacher may have to provide information about the history of the local area during the chosen time period or arrange for a local history expert to visit the class to help the pupils understand the important events that have taken place in their local area.

Facts and information about the area could be made part of an ongoing display of work so that the display can develop into an information database that all the pupils can share.

Pupils could work in groups to find out about the history of the local area and its buildings.

**Using the 'Summary guide'**

Writing a summary helps pupils to select and use relevant information rather than just downloading information from the internet or photocopying text and not really understanding what it is all about. The 'Summary guide' ensures that the pupil understands how to structure a summary and what the purpose of it is.

Read the guide with the pupils and discuss the differences between a summary and a more extended piece of writing. A word limit could be set.

**Using the 'Character map'**

This sheet enables the pupils to plan the character for their story. It helps to remind them to consider all aspects of the character's personality and behaviour and how they might use language to describe him or her.

Go through the sheet with the pupils and ensure they understand that they are writing about an invented character, not a real person.

**Using the 'Story map'**

This sheet enables the pupils to plan out their story in detail before writing it. The questions on the sheet help to remind the pupils to include historical facts in their story.

Discuss the sheet with the pupils, making sure they understand what they have to do.

### 3 Other points to note

Firm deadlines should be provided to help the pupils develop their priorities when researching for information and planning their writing.

The teacher's role for 'Task sheet 2' is to help the pupils plan their story so that it incorporates aspects of their research about the local area's history. How will their invented character fit into the chosen time period? What type of work, living conditions and daily routines would be appropriate? Perhaps the character could be part of a special event that happened in the area. The able pupil should enjoy meeting the challenge of writing a story that incorporates accurate historical evidence and produce some interesting writing. Less able pupils could be supported by carrying out a more directed task, such as writing a story entitled 'A Day in the Life of…'

## Links to the National Curriculum

### English – Speaking and Listening

*Level 5: Pupils choose material that is relevant to the topic and speaks to engage the interest of the reader.*
*Level 6: Pupils speak audibly, clearly and fluently adapting their conversation to the demands of the different contexts.*

### English – Reading

*Level 5: Pupils read a range of text, printed and ICT based to select and use information appropriately.*
*Level 6: Pupils engage with challenging material and subject matter.*
*They identify layers of meaning and comment on their significance.*

### English – Writing

*Level 5: Pupils write using imaginative vocabulary and words precisely.*
*Writing structure shows simple and complex sentences and use of paragraphs.*
*Level 6: Pupils' writing engages and sustains the reader's interest.*
*They plan, draft and edit work to produce an extended narrative.*

### History

*Level 5: Pupils show factual knowledge and understanding of aspects of British history.*
*They describe features of past society, events and people in a given context.*
*They evaluate and use sources of information effectively.*
*Level 6: Pupils use factual knowledge to describe past societies and events.*
*Information is selected and organised to produce work set.*

## Links to Literacy Framework

### Year 6, Term 3

### Word level work

*W3 – to use dictionaries and IT spellchecks.*

### Sentence level work

*S1 – to revise language conventions and grammatical features of narratives.*

### Text level work

*T9 – to write summaries.*
*T14 – to write an extended story, worked on over time on a theme identified in reading.*

# Assessment sheet

Name: _____  Date: _____

| | Achieved | To achieve |
|---|---|---|

## Speaking and Listening:

**Level 5:**
- Chooses material that is relevant to the topic and speaks to engage the interest of the listener.

**Level 6:**
- Speaks audibly, clearly and fluently, adapting the conversation to the demands of the different contexts.

## Reading:

**Level 5:**
- Reads a range of texts, printed and ICT based to select and use information appropriately.

**Level 6:**
- Engages with challenging material and subject matter.
- Identifies layers of meaning and comments on their significance.

## Writing:

**Level 5:**
- Writes using imaginative vocabulary and words precisely.
- Writing structure shows simple and complex sentences and use of paragraphs.

**Level 6:**
- Plans, drafts and edits work to produce an extended narrative.

## History:

**Level 5:**
- Shows factual knowledge and understanding of aspects of British history.
- Describes features of past society, events and people in a given context.
- Evaluates and uses sources of information effectively.

**Level 6:**
- Uses factual knowledge to describe past societies and events.

# Task sheet 1

## Finding out about where you live

### Aim

To find out about the history of the place where you live.

### Tasks

- Use the **My action planning sheet** to help you plan your work.

- **Make a list** of all the facts you know about the area where you live. This can be part of a village, town, city or county – your teacher will tell you which one to choose.

- **Find out** about your local area during the time period your teacher suggests. (This might be during the Victorian times, Tudor times, Roman times or 1930s to 1940s, for example.) Find out how people lived and worked during this time.

- **Discuss** with someone in your group the important events during this time period and say what interests you about them. Share your ideas about how people lived at that time. What would you have liked or disliked about living in that time?

- Look at the buildings in your local area. Were any of them built during the chosen time period? Choose three of them and find out what they were used for then and what they are used for now.

- **Write a summary** of what you have found out. **Use the Summary guide** to help you.

# Task sheet 2

## Writing a story

### Aim

To plan and write a story about an invented character based on your research into a specific time period in your local area.

### Tasks

- Continue to use the **My action planning sheet** to help you plan your work.

- **Discuss** with someone in your group the things you found out about your local area during the chosen time period. Share ideas about the types of people who may have lived and worked there then.

- **Invent** a character who could have lived in your local area during the chosen time period. Use the **Character map** to help you plan out everything about this character – his or her name and age, what he or she looks like, where he or she lives, what work he or she does and what he or she is like.

  What is my character like?

- **Think** about something that might happen to this character. **Plan** a story based on what happens. Use the **Story map** to help you.

- **Remember** – the story must be set in the chosen time period in your local area so everything you write about should be relevant to that time period.

- **Edit** your work and **write** your final draft.

## Extension work

- Illustrate a cover for your story that shows where your character lives or works.

- Design an advertisement for an entertainment that might have taken place in the past in your local area.

# Planning guidelines

## What to do

1. Read the task sheets carefully and then make up your action plan of tasks to do and when to do them by completing the 'My action planning sheet'. Identify the skills you will demonstrate when carrying out the tasks. Are there any skills you need help with?

2. Use the 'Resources' sheet to help you find out about the history of your local area during the chosen time period. If your family has lived in this area for a long time, they may be very helpful to your research.

3. When finding out about how people lived and worked you may not be able to find information that relates to your local area in particular – you may need to use more general information about the time period.

4. You should be able to find out more specific information about the buildings in your area. The local museum or archives should be able to help you.

5. Remember – when inventing your character for your story, make him or her as realistic for the time period as possible. Refer to your summary to help you determine the type of clothing, houses and work that your character may have experienced. Use archive information to think of an appropriate name for your character. Complete all sections of the 'Character map' to ensure you have thought about all aspects of your character.

6. Decide how your character is going to be woven into a story. Will he or she be part of an actual event that took place in your local area? Make sure all the facts you use in your story are based on the research you have carried out. Try and make the story as realistic as possible. Make the reader imagine what it was like to live in that period of history.

7. Share your story with someone in your group. How realistic do they think it is? How could it be improved? Edit your story to make it fit the chosen time more accurately.

8. Make a final version of your story. You may want to illustrate it.

# Resources

The local area

| Internet | Local history:<br>www.domesdaybook.co.uk<br>www.bbc.co.uk/history/lj/localj/index.html<br>Normans:<br>www.spartacus.schoolnet.co.uk/Normans.htm<br>Tudors:<br>www.links4kids.co.uk/tudors.htm<br>http://tudorhistory.org<br>Victorians:<br>www.bbc.co.uk/schools/victorians/teachers/useful.shtml<br>www.schoolhistory.co.uk/primarylinks/victorian.html<br>Literacy: new words/word origins<br>www.domesdaybook.co.uk/glossary.html<br>www.domesdaybook.co.uk/book.html | Try CD-Rom encyclopaedias. |
|---|---|---|
| Speakers and other sources | Speakers from the local history society, Business people who work in an old building may have records of its history. Newspapers hold records of news which might help your research. | Contact by writing or phoning. |
| Libraries | Non-fiction reference texts and history books will be helpful. CDs and videos may be available. | The librarian will help you. |
| Visits | Visits to local places of interest, buildings, museums or churches may be helpful and interesting. | These can be individual or group visits. Discuss places to visit with friends. |
| Audience | Friends and people who have lived in the area a long time may know about its history. | |
| Your own ideas | Map out your ideas and check them in detail against your research findings. Are your facts correct and descriptions accurate? | Discuss your ideas with friends and your teacher. |

**100 Literacy**
*Challenges*

# Summary guide

## The local area

A summary is a short piece of writing that consists of a brief statement of the main points of information that you feel are needed for the reader.

A summary is written in sentences and short paragraphs. Each new paragraph develops the points you are making in a logical sequence.

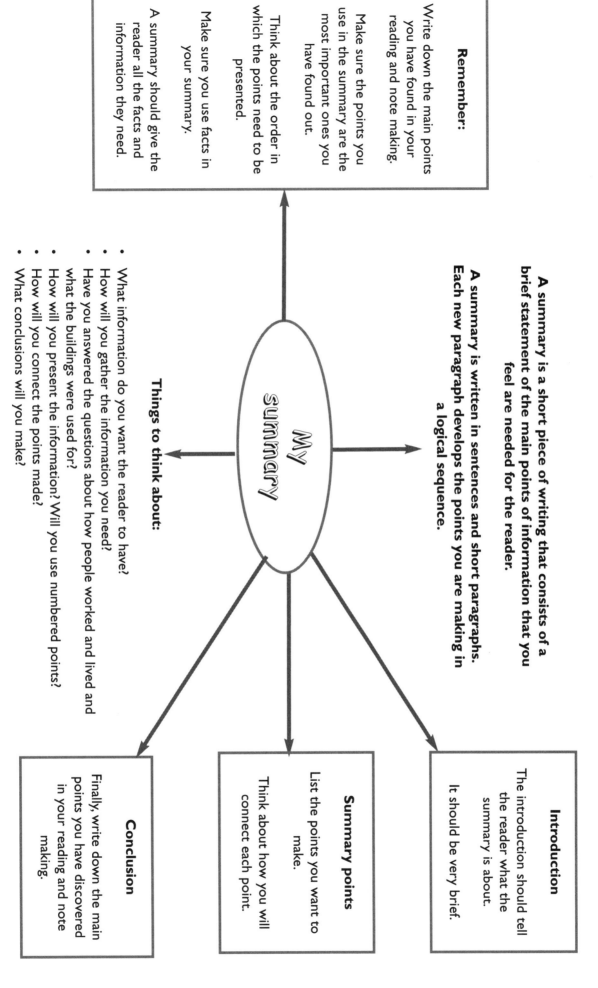

### Remember:

Write down the main points you have found in your reading and note making.

Make sure the points you use in the summary are the most important ones you have found out.

Think about the order in which the points need to be presented.

Make sure you use facts in your summary.

A summary should give the reader all the facts and information they need.

### Things to think about:

- What information do you want the reader to have?
- How will you gather the information you need?
- Have you answered the questions about how people worked and lived and what the buildings were used for?
- How will you present the information? Will you use numbered points?
- How will you connect the points made?
- What conclusions will you make?

**My summary**

### Introduction

The introduction should tell the reader what the summary is about.

It should be very brief.

### Summary points

List the points you want to make.

Think about how you will connect each point.

### Conclusion

Finally, write down the main points you have discovered in your reading and note making.

## How will you use language?

To describe the character ☐

To help develop the plot ☐

To give facts ☐

To show emotions ☐

To use imagery ☐
(words that put ideas into our minds about the characters)

## Reader's response

What do you want to tell the reader and how do you want them to feel?

_____
_____
_____
_____

## What will be your purpose as the writer?

To tell a story ☐

To inform about life at that time in history ☐

To make us think about the issues raised ☐

What does he or she do? _____

Where does he or she live? _____

What happens to him or her in the story? _____

### Character's name:

Fact file

**Age** _____

**Male/Female** _____

**Time period** _____

**Personality – the character could be:**

| | |
|---|---|
| outgoing | selfish |
| kind | good tempered |
| bad tempered | stubborn |
| caring | friendly |
| trustworthy | honest |
| sly | a bully |

Add your own ideas:
_____
_____
_____

## Story title

### What language will you use?

Narrative – to tell the story ☐

Descriptive – to set the scene ☐

Factual – to provide historical information ☐

1st or 3rd person ☐

### Type of story

Historical ☐

Adventure ☐

Mystery ☐

Other _____

### Reader's response

Will the reader feel the way you want them to feel about your character?

What do you want them to think?

### Content

**Beginning** – this sets the scene and introduces the character.

**Development** – this sets out a problem or adventure the character has.

**Resolution** – this explains how the problem or adventure is solved or ends.

**Ending** – this explains what happens to the character in the end.

### Themes and issues:

Do you have a message to give to the reader about what life was like for your character in the time you are writing about?

Think about the relationships people had with each other in the time you are writing about.

Was life fair for everyone? How does your character cope?

### Historical research

List the facts you will need to use and make notes on the way people lived at that time.

When you write your story make sure you set the scene using your historical research so that your story will be believable to the reader.

# Challenge 10

# Musical tour

## Teacher's notes

### Purposes

- To gain an understanding of the geography of Europe including the physical make-up of the different countries.
- To learn about the musical culture of Europe.
- To link the music of a culture with the place and environment.
- To develop thinking, planning and time management skills.

### Aims

- To find out about the music of three countries in Europe.
- To prepare and present a talk that uses music and pictures to tell others about three European countries – a musical guided tour.

### Resources required

The pupil will need copies of the following:

| | | |
|---|---|---|
| 1 | 'Challenge sheet' | page 112 |
| 2 | 'My action planning sheet' | page 113 |
| 3 | 'Task sheets' | pages 107 and 108 |
| 4 | 'Planning guidelines' | page 109 |
| 5 | 'Resources' sheet | page 110 |
| 6 | 'Map of Europe' | page 111 |
| 7 | 'Skills sheets' | pages 114–117 |

The pupils will also need access to atlases and the music of European composers.

### The teacher's role

#### 1 Introducing the challenge

Write the following in the top box of a copy of the 'Challenge sheet' (page 112):

*You are going to use maps and other information sources to find out about the countries of Europe. You are to choose three of these countries and find out about the music and composers that represent these countries.*

*You are then going to prepare and present a talk that uses music and pictures to tell others about your chosen countries.*

Then photocopy the 'Challenge sheet' and give it to the pupils. Alternatively, they could be given a blank copy of the sheet and write the challenge on it themselves. It is important for them to have the challenge to refer to.

#### 2 Providing support for the task sheets

**Finding out about the countries of Europe**

This part of the challenge (see 'Task sheet 1') could be carried out as a whole class activity. The more able pupils should be able to research the physical geography and use atlases without too much help, whereas other pupils may need more support. An up-to-date map of Europe displayed on the class wall would be a useful reference point for the pupils. (The map on page 111 may need to be enlarged for the children to write the names of the countries on it.)

Introduce the idea of how physical features like mountains, rivers and plains give a country its character and influences the way people live and develop. Use music to represent the make-up of some of the countries. For example, the music of Sibelius – 'Finlandia' might conjure up a vision of deep fjords and high mountains, whereas the music of Strauss might lead the listener to envisage a lively, busy country.

Below are listed some well known composers and their countries:

> Finland – Sibelius; Norway – Grieg; France – Bizet, Saint Saëns, Ravel; Germany – Bach, Beethoven, Brahms, Handel (who went to England to live), Offenbach (who went to live in France); Poland – Chopin; Czechoslovakia (Czech Republic and Slovakia) – Dvorak, Smetana; Britain – Elgar, Delius (who moved to France), Purcell, Holst, Walton; Austria – Mozart, Strauss; Italy – Paganini, Verdi, Rossini; Hungary – Liszt; Russia – Rachmaninov, Stravinsky, Tchaikovsky.

#### 3 Other points to note

The activities on both task sheets could be carried out as whole class activities with the teacher providing the class with the necessary background information and music for three of the countries. The more able, however, should be able to research information about the countries, their music and composers themselves, depending on the resources available to them. The able pupils should also be able to present a talk that will interest the listener and show understanding of the physical geography of the chosen countries.

The display of work produced by the pupils as part of 'Task sheet 1' will allow others in the class to gain an insight into the various countries of Europe.

Note – the bands of the armed forces travel around Europe and it may be possible to arrange for them to visit the school to give a performance and to talk to the pupils about the music they play/hear as they travel around.

## Links to the National Curriculum

### English – Speaking and Listening

*Level 5: Pupils listen and talk confidently to others. They make contributions that are relevant to the topic.*
*Level 6: Pupils adapt their talk to the demands of the topic set confidently. They take a full part in discussion and listen to the contributions of others.*

### English – Reading

*Level 5: Pupils retrieve and collate information from different sources.*
*Level 6: Pupils show that they are able to summarise a range of information from different sources.*

### English – Writing

*Level 5: Pupils' writing is adapted to the task and is varied and interesting.*
*Level 6: Pupils' writing explores ideas and engages the reader's interest.*

### Geography

*Level 5: Themes – pupils study places and environments and gain a knowledge of the location of places in Europe. They can describe and explain geographical patterns.*
*Level 6: Pupils describe a range of physical processes and understand how places fit within a wider geographical context.*

### Music

*Level 5: Pupils can explore and respond to a range of non-musical starting points. They can appreciate a range of live and recorded music from different times and cultures.*
*They can identify how time and place can influence the way music is created, performed and heard.*
*Level 6: Pupils identify and explore the different processes and contents of selected musical genres and styles. They analyse, compare and evaluate how music reflects the contexts in which it is created and performed.*

## Links to Literacy Framework
### Year 6, Term 3

**Word level work**
*W3 – to use dictionaries and IT spellchecks.*

**Sentence level work**
*S4 – to secure control of complex sentences.*

**Text level work**
*T18 – to secure the skills of skimming, scanning and efficient reading so that research is fast and effective.*
*T22 – to select the appropriate style and form to suit a specific purpose and audience.*

# Assessment sheet

Name:_____ Date: _____

| | Achieved | To achieve |
|---|---|---|
| **Speaking and Listening:**<br><br>**Level 5:**<br>• Makes contributions relevant to the topic.<br><br>**Level 6:**<br>• Talk is adapted to the demands of the topic during presentation.<br><br>**Reading:**<br><br>**Level 5:**<br>• Retrieves and collates information successfully.<br><br>**Level 6:**<br>• Can summarise a range of information from various sources.<br><br>**Writing:**<br><br>**Level 5:**<br>• Writing is appropriate for the task set.<br><br>**Level 6:**<br>• Writing explores ideas and engages the reader's interest.<br><br>**Geography:**<br><br>**Level 5:**<br>• Studies places and environments. Shows knowledge of locations in Europe.<br>• Can describe and explain a geographical pattern.<br><br>**Level 6:**<br>• Shows knowledge of places in Europe and how the environment can influence attitudes and ideas.<br><br>**Music:**<br><br>**Level 5:**<br>• Can explore a range of non-music starting points.<br>• Shows how time and place can influence the way music is heard and performed.<br><br>**Level 6:**<br>• Identifies and explores different contexts of musical genres and styles. | | |

# Task sheet 1

## Finding out about the countries of Europe

### Aim
To find out about the music of three countries in Europe.

### Tasks

- Use the **My action planning sheet** to help you plan your work.

- Using an atlas, **find the names of the countries of Europe** and write them on the blank map provided.

- **Select three of these countries** and **find out the names of their important composers** and a piece of music they have composed.

- Find out what the countries are like geographically. For example, do they have mountains, rivers or plains?

- **Make a map** of each of your three countries showing their most important physical features. For example, a map of Austria might show the location and names of the most important mountains and lakes.

- **Listen to the music** of the composers you have found. Does their music help you imagine what their countries are like? Write a paragraph explaining what each piece of music is about.

- Listen to one of the pieces of music and **draw or find pictures** that show what the music tells you.

- **Make a display** of your maps and pictures of the three countries you have selected. Tell others in your group what you have found out about the countries and their music so far.

# Task sheet 2

## Preparing a talk

### Aim

To prepare and present a talk, using music and pictures, to tell others about three countries in Europe – a musical guided tour.

### Tasks

• Continue to use the **My action planning sheet** to help you plan your work.

• **Discuss** your findings about your three European countries and their music with others in your group. Are there any similarities? What is different about the countries and their music?

• **Pretend** that you are actually going to visit your three chosen countries – **plan** an **itinerary**. Which one would you visit first? How would you get there? How would you get from one country to the next one?

• **Use** your route plan to help you structure your talk.

• Use the piece of music and the pictures from Task sheet 1 as part of your talk.

• **Draft** your talk. **Practise** it in order to time your presentation.

• **Edit** your work and **write** your final draft.

• **Present** your talk.

## Extension work

• Choose a piece of music from a European country and make up a poem to go with it.

• Write a story to match a piece of music.

# Planning guidelines

## What to do:

1. Read the task sheets carefully and then make up your action plan of tasks to do and when to do them by completing the 'My action planning sheet'. Identify the skills you will demonstrate when carrying out the tasks. Are there any skills you need help with?

2. Use the 'Resources' sheet to help you find out about the three countries you have chosen.

3. When drawing your maps, remember to do them in pencil first so that corrections can be easily made. You might like to use an overhead projector to present your maps. Ask your teacher to help you.

4. Your family and friends may be able to help you find music from your chosen countries.

5. Remember when planning your route to think about the best way to travel from one country to another. Will you fly, go by train or go by car? Which will be the best way to see the country you are passing through?

6. Decide how long your chosen extract of music will be and what pictures you will use to show what the country is like. The words from your presentation will have to fit in with the music and pictures you use.

7. Think about the visual presentation of your talk:

   a) You can decide to present a visually different map of Europe by making a model, if you wish.

   b) You may prefer to illustrate a map blank with your pictures. You can always make the map A3 size.

   c) You may use a series of pictures and images to represent each country as it is travelled through.

8. Make sure you practise your presentation and change it if you need to.

# Resources

| Internet | http://www.classical.net/music/mstrindx.html | Try CD-Rom encyclopaedias. |
|---|---|---|
| **Speakers and other sources** | Local musicians or European visitors can tell you about the music of their country.<br><br>BBC music archives; Classic FM. Embassies will send information. | Contact by writing or phoning. |
| **Libraries** | Reference sections, specialist music sections, geography sections. | The librarian will help you. |
| **Visits** | Music concerts or a visit to an embassy.<br><br>A trip to Europe!<br><br>Local travel agents may help with information. | These can be individual or group visits. |
| **Audience** | Ask friends and family what sort of music they associate with visiting countries in Europe – they may give you ideas. | Discuss places to visit with friends. |
| **Your own ideas** | Jot down all your ideas about the places you have visited or might like to visit in Europe. | Discuss your ideas with friends and your teacher. |

Musical tour

# Map of Europe

# Challenge sheet

The challenge:

Name: _____

Start date: _____

Completion date: _____

My comments about the completed task:

Teacher's comments:

# My action planning sheet

| Date to start task | Task to be carried out and by whom | Date to complete task |
|---|---|---|
| | | |

# Skills sheet – 1

Name: _____ Date: _____

| | I can do this | I need more help to do this |
|---|---|---|

## Speaking and Listening – I can:

- listen to people and talk to them about the topic we are working on.
- say what my ideas are about the topic.
- evaluate information and discuss it:
    - in a pair
    - in a group
- explain, report and evaluate ideas when talking:
    - in a group
    - with a partner
- discuss how language is used to give meaning to ideas.
- read aloud confidently.
- speak using appropriate words to communicate my ideas.
- discuss a fiction or non-fiction text with:
    - a partner
    - a group
- use the words in a text to explain my ideas about the text.
- use the text to choose material that is helpful to my work.
- present information to an audience.
- speak in a way that is interesting to others.

## Reading – I can:

- read aloud correctly and well.
- select information I need from a text.
- use information from a text in my speaking and listening and writing tasks.
- identify words, phrases and sentences in a text that help me to understand it better.
- identify characters and setting in a text.
- choose appropriate material for my task.
- identify and use specialist vocabulary.
- identify how words are used in different texts.
- scan read a text for information.

# Skills sheet – 2

Name: _____ Date: _____

| | I can do this | I need more help to do this |
|---|---|---|

- identify facts and opinions in a text.
- explain how words and sentences are used to help the reader understand the text.
- read and understand different types of fiction and non-fiction texts.
- use dictionaries, encyclopaedias and ICT to find information that I need for my work.

## Writing – I can:

- draft, edit and write for a particular purpose and in the correct format: a letter, a journal, a report, a story, a leaflet, a script, a book review, a discussion text, a summary.
- use writing maps and guides to help me to plan, edit and redraft my work.
- make notes on a topic.
- design work using an appropriate layout: leaflet, a newspaper article, an advert, a display of information.
- use words in an interesting way when I write.
- write for different readers, using appropriate language so they will understand my writing.
- write using simple and complex sentences.
- present my writing in neat and clearly joined handwriting.
- use punctuation correctly.
- spell most of the words I use in my writing correctly.

## Maths – I can:

- use number operations to solve problems.
- use number operations in 'real life' situations, such as working out the cost of an activity.

## History – I can:

- use history texts to research for information.
- make notes using history texts.
- describe events in history and explain what I have learned about them.

# Skills sheet – 3

Name: _____ Date: _____

|  | I can do this | I need more help to do this |
|---|---|---|

- use the facts I have researched in my writing.
- use information to make notes for my tasks.
- investigate how people lived their lives at different times in history.

## Geography – I can:

- identify where places are on a map.
- describe what different places are like.
- describe the physical features of different countries in Europe.
- mark on a blank map where European countries are.

## ICT – I can:

- use a variety of audio-visual aids to help me to complete my tasks.
- use desktop publishing to design and produce work such as leaflets, advertisements and games.
- organise text and images using ICT.
- use ICT to find information that I need.
- produce my work using different ICT packages.
- use ICT to plan work for a particular audience.
- use ICT to plan, save, edit and produce my final piece of work.

## Science – I can:

- research for information using science texts.
- make notes after reading of science texts.
- show that I understand life processes and living things by talking, reading and writing about them.
- use scientific information in my writing.
- show how the environment affects animals and people.
- explain what nutrition is.
- use scientific information to show how activity keeps the body healthy.

# Skills sheet – 4

Name: _____ Date: _____

| | I can do this | I need more help to do this |
|---|---|---|
| **PSHE –** | | |

**PSHE –**

Through talking, reading, researching and writing I can:

show what makes a healthy lifestyle;

show how healthy eating is good for people;

show how exercise is important for keeping fit;

show I understand the problems of the elderly;

find information about their problems;

listen to explanations of the problems of the elderly;

show understanding of moral and social problems;

show I respect the elderly.

**Art –** I can:

• select visual and other information to plan images for stories, music, adverts and posters.

• use different materials and processes to present my ideas visually.

• present visual information for different people.

**Music –** I can:

• use different starting points for my research.

• present music from different times and places to a chosen group of people.

• select different music for different times and cultures.

• explain why I like listening to different pieces of music.

• explain my musical choices to different people.

**P.E. –** I can:

• explain why regular exercise is good for me.

• do different exercises that will keep me fit.